"Through her darkest nights to her brightest mornings, God had a plan all along! Our sis Pat does an incredible job of allowing us into her pain so we can rejoice in her glory! We pray this book will touch the lives of many!"

—Sherice and Tim Brown, former NFL player, member of the Pro Football Hall of Fame, and Heisman Trophy winner

"We are touched by Pat Smith's faithfulness to God's directives in her life, and know that He will use her story to demonstrate to others His rock solid faithfulness to His children."

—Janet and Tony Dorsett, former NFL player, member of the Pro Football Hall of Fame, and Heisman Trophy winner

"*Second Chances* is a book that brilliantly and honestly tells a story about redemption. My sister Pat will take you on a beautiful journey that will lead you from a place of hopelessness to healing . . . and from pain to God's promise and purpose for your life."

—Joy Hill, first lady of The Potter's House of Denver

"Pat Smith shows a bravery in her new book that will encourage even the strongest. From a difficult and painful divorce in Los Angeles to finding love and happiness in Dallas, you will identify with a woman who has fought the odds to find her purpose and now gives to others freely."

—Matrice and Ron Kirk, former United States trade representative, Texas secretary of state, and mayor of Dallas

"Each time I am with Pat, I am overcome with awe and admiration. Her desire to change the lives of others is a true testimony to her profound courage and faith. When you read *Second Chances*, I have no doubt that you will be as impressed and inspired as I have been with her strength."

—Robin McGraw, philanthropist, entrepreneur, television personality, and two-time #1 *New York Times* bestselling author

"My friend Pat Smith's new book, *Second Chances*, is an honest and moving account of her journey from loss to redemption. I encourage you to read this book, let it inspire you, and then allow God to replace your ashes with beauty and your sorrow with joy."

—Victoria Osteen, co-pastor of Lakewood Church

"If you believe second chances only happen to other people, let Pat's story, the lessons she so courageously shares, and the faith she found help you recognize that hope is here for you, too. You can choose faith over fear. This book is like a jolt of wisdom and inspiration that can help you find your strength and the courage to change your own story."

—Christi Paul, CNN *New Day* weekend anchor and author,
Love Isn't Supposed to Hurt

"When you first see Pat you are struck by her outer beauty. She is stunning! But you would really be missing out if you didn't read this book to discover that she is even more beautiful on the inside. She is transparent and makes herself vulnerable by sharing her stories of setbacks and recoveries in the book, and you will see that her heart is on a beautiful mission to help other women. I know she will inspire you like she has inspired me."

—Kimberly Schlegel Whitman, editor-at-large,
Southern Living, author, and lifestyle expert

"A captivating read that will give any woman the strength to stand up tall . . . again."

—Kym Whitley, comedienne, film and TV actress,
and star of *Raising Whitley*

SECOND
CHANCES

FINDING HEALING *for* YOUR PAIN,
REGAINING YOUR STRENGTH,
CELEBRATING YOUR NEW LIFE

PAT SMITH

BETHANYHOUSE

a division of Baker Publishing Group
Minneapolis, Minnesota

Published by Bethany House Publishers
11400 Hampshire Avenue South
Bloomington, Minnesota 55438
www.bethanyhouse.com

Bethany House Publishers is a division of
Baker Publishing Group, Grand Rapids, Michigan

Printed in the United States of America

Library of Congress Control Number: 2016930584

ISBN 978-0-7642-1284-0

Cover design by Peter Gloege | LOOK Design Studio

Front cover photography by Brian Braun

Author is represented by Dupree/Miller & Associates.

16 17 18 19 20 21 22   7 6 5 4 3 2 1

This book is dedicated in memory of the most beautiful
woman on the inside and out I've ever known,
my mother, Mildred Page Southall,
who went home to be with the Lord
when I was only twenty-two. I created an
award in her honor called Page's Angel.

A special dedication is given to a woman
who exemplifies my mother's heart for giving
and perseverance through life's struggles and setbacks.
This woman aspires to help others
who have overcome setbacks,
and shares her resources freely.

Faye C. Briggs is the most perfect "Imperfect Princess"
and 2014 Page's Angel Award recipient.
Faye listened to the call from God to build a home that
welcomes thousands of people a year to raise dollars for
others in need of a second chance.
This inspires me that God gives us all
second chances if we honor Him.
She is a special angel to me.

Contents

Contents

Foreword

We knew when we first met Pat Smith that she was going to be a special vessel for God. She was soon to be a new bride to Emmitt and was learning how to navigate the Dallas Cowboys' Wives' Club along with a brand-new city of opportunity. Pat was strong in her faith but new to her calling to minister God's Word.

Her first years attending The Potter's House were quiet. She flourished undetected as she sat in the pew each Sunday listening to God's Word and applying the messages to her life. Pat came to Dallas having survived many disappointments and setbacks: the loss of her mother to breast cancer, losing the Miss USA Pageant, and a difficult failed first marriage to a high-profile entertainer. She was carrying a heavy load, lightened by her love for Emmitt, but still weighed down as she was trying to find her own voice and connect with new people.

We always knew that God would turn her pain into purpose, and we told her so. Watching her map out a vision for her non-profit, Treasure You, has been a delight. Witnessing firsthand her service to so many others as she embraces her ministry has been an honor to us.

Her book, *Second Chances*, is inspired by her experiences and her desire to encourage others through some of their darkest moments. She shares stories of loss, pain, and disappointment resolved by God's forgiveness and faithfulness. Reading some of the stories, you will feel the heartbreak of the women and want to hold them until their fears subside. When you are finished reading the book, you will be reminded that God is so real and that His mercies are new every morning.

Beholding the beauty of Pat's obedience to God's calling has been a blessing to us personally and to The Potter's House family.

—Bishop and Mrs. T.D. Jakes Sr.

Introduction

I wasn't good enough.

That's what I used to think. For decades, I felt like a failure. I questioned why certain things kept happening in my life. I wallowed when things didn't go my way.

Until one day, when I realized that all of my pain and hurt was really an *opportunity*.

Second chances are about forgiveness, reconciliation, new beginnings, rebirth, renewal, freedom, and redemption. Once you realize that your journey is all about these strands of second chances, you can appreciate and be grateful for them.

As I look back, I see two distinct times in my life when people I knew only on a business level called out the fact that they saw my life as a "journey of second chances." Second chances? That resonated with me. I don't believe in coincidences, so to have two different people see this in me meant something. As soon as my eyes were open to the idea that my life was full of second chances, I saw second-chance moments celebrated everywhere—on TV, in magazine stories, in church . . . For a long time, I knew I was supposed to do something in my life

11

related to second chances. But for years I didn't know what. Until I founded Treasure You.

A few years ago I hosted a Treasure You event with Robin Roberts. It was called "Celebrating Second Chances with Overcomers." I want to explain how the name came to be. As I studied the women whom we were honoring, I saw that each had been given second chances in her life. Each of these women had been through extreme adversity, and they were turning their pain into purpose. I just knew that's what my event was about.

Some of us experience poignant, strong, and powerful moments that define a second chance. But second chances are also those simple moments where God gives you an opportunity. It's up to you to recognize this opportunity to do something better, persevere, reconcile a relationship, give thanks, affect and impact others' lives, grow tougher or stronger, build endurance . . . and grow closer to God. It wasn't until I was writing this book that I realized the defining moment of my second chance: *giving my life over to Christ.* Your second chance may become clear in another way. Every person is different. Every person has his or her own number of second chances. And sometimes it takes time to even realize that God has given you one.

I had no idea that God was setting me up for second chances.

Oftentimes we are so focused on the negatives, hurt, or bad decisions from our past that we don't recognize the opportunity our past has given us. Look at me! Once I understood that we all get second chances, I felt a sense of hope. For so long I couldn't make sense of my journey. Now, through the grace of God, I can.

My hope in writing this book is to free people from their pain and bondage and help them realize the power that comes out of suffering, disappointment, loss, and hurt. God is the God of second chances. If you can grab ahold of that understanding, honor Him and hold fast to Him, have faith and stay true to Him, you too will receive second chances.

I believe in keeping it real and taking off the mask, so it was important to me from the day I began writing this book to be as open as possible. This book is an opportunity for sharing. One of my favorite parts of our Treasure You retreats is the pajama party. We ask everyone to put on their comfy pajamas, take off their makeup, remove their masks, get rid of all pretentiousness, and let down their guard. I'm hoping this experience is re-created as you read each word. Let us connect from heart to heart. I'm vulnerable in these pages, and I challenge you to join me in that vulnerability with open and honest thoughts and emotions. I pray that you see your past does impact your future, but it's up to you to do the work and release any anger, hurt, pain, or disappointment you carry so that you can receive your second chance, feel free of shame or guilt, and impact others' lives for God's glory. I pray that if you don't already recognize a second-chance moment, you will after reading this book. I pray that your second-chance moment impacts your life and your relationship with Christ—and impacts others for good, too.

So I invite you to put on your pj's, light a candle, and prepare a cup of coffee or tea. Settle in and get comfortable. When you're ready, turn the page. And let's share what I call a "Treasure You" moment.

ONE
Unstuck

Life is all about seasons. And, perhaps more important, how we grow from them.

In my twenties, I was married to Martin Lawrence. While our marriage didn't last for the long term, we both have come full circle in our relationship. No one gets divorced from a lack of relationship problems, but we have since worked through our issues, and today we're the best of friends. We have a daughter whom we have watched grow into a strong, loving woman of God. Our families adore each other. My children call him Daddy Martin and his kids call me Mommy Pat. My husband and Martin are dear friends. Our families spend time together, take trips together, and live life together.

In short, there's nothing Martin and I wouldn't do for each other.

But like I said, life is about seasons, and years ago as a young Southern girl from Virginia working in Governor Douglas Wilder's office and dreaming of hosting a national morning network news show, I had no idea how quickly life would change.

In a blink, I was in Los Angeles, married to a popular movie star, residing in a Beverly Hills home, and living life in the spotlight. There were parties and premieres, designer dresses and celebrity friends. It might seem as if I were on top of the world.

But the golden path was tarnished.

I met Martin Lawrence at one of his comedy shows in Virginia. Onstage, he was raw, edgy, and hilarious. I felt a little crush coming on. My girlfriend and I had backstage passes, and as soon as he and I were introduced, we had conflict. I'd never met anyone like him. It was exciting. My girlfriend and I went to the club where the after-party was happening. It wasn't long before we had an exchange that turned into a disagreement, and I walked away that night thinking that I wouldn't ever see him again. But as fate would have it, as I was leaving the club, I bumped into Martin's brother, Robert. We had a great conversation. "You're cool," he said. "My brother needs to call you. You two should talk. Let me give him your number."

If he hadn't asked for my number, my relationship with Martin would've ended right then.

Martin called, and away from the fans and club scene, something happened. We connected. We talked all night. I can remember my sweet roommate Trish asking me to keep it down a little. I couldn't help myself. Martin had me laughing—actually he had me cracking up!

Over the next year, we dated on and off. *On* when I visited him in L.A. and fell in love. *Off* when we drifted apart and he got engaged to another woman. Then *on* again after he broke off the engagement and we spent time together to reconnect. By this time, after placing first runner-up in the Miss USA pageant (or second loser as I called it), I had made the difficult decision to resign from my position with the governor's office and move to L.A. to pursue my television career. I guess the timing was right. Martin and I spent an amazing week together, inseparable and happy. It wasn't long after that I was standing on the rooftop of his home as he got down on his knee and proposed.

Right away we started to plan. At this point, I was pursuing my career and taking care of the wedding details, and Martin was in Miami filming *Bad Boys*. It was a crazy, harried time, and that meant a crazy, harried engagement. We were the same couple who fought the night we met, and we lived up to that low standard throughout our engagement.

When I met and fell in love with Martin, I fell hard. I was so enamored with him. When we weren't in conflict with each other, he made me laugh. He made me feel special. He filled a void and gave me a feeling of security, one that had been lacking since my mother died. She had been so strong and prominent in my life, and I liked her having so much control over my decisions. When she was gone, I was lost. I had been desperately looking for something to fill her void, but instead of turning to God and allowing Him to heal me, I turned to Martin and expected him to repair that hole in my heart.

For a while he did an excellent job. He made life fun, and I became distracted from having to deal with the pain of my loss because this little country girl from Virginia was now living in L.A. and attending Hollywood premieres of major movies, and doing it all on the arm of the man I loved. However, fun and exciting doesn't necessary translate into a good, lifelong decision. If my mother had been alive, I believe she would've helped me see that getting married so quickly was going to be an enormous mistake.

Martin and I were young, passionate, and impulsive. We entered marriage without giving it much thought. We ignored the warning signs: the fights, the rocky courtship, the travel, and our personality differences. We went with our strong feelings for each other and bought into the idea that it just felt right to

say "I do." We figured everything else would simply work itself
out once we were married.

But it didn't.

We had happy times, but we had some really bad times, too.
And happy moments could turn bad very quickly. I felt as though
we were both walking on eggshells, trying not to upset each
other most of the time, which led to unhealthy interactions.

I knew things had to change—especially after we had our
beautiful baby girl, Jasmin. I kept trying to make it work. I was
willing to tolerate whatever it took to stay together, doing whatever I could to create a happy home. We never attended church
together, prayed together, or studied God's Word together, even
though we both grew up in families that loved God. I now know
that practicing faith is the foundation of marriage. We were
struggling to make it work by our own power, but marriage
can only be sustained by God's power! I didn't want to go to
church alone. I quit going to church altogether. I quit believing
I was worthy of love. And I quit believing there would ever be
a happily-ever-after.

Though I put on a brave mask in the public eye, things grew
progressively worse behind closed doors. I was fearful to stay
alone so my sister, Pam, often stayed the night with me when
Martin traveled. Then one night, after Martin had been away, he
came home unexpectedly, and we got into an argument. Things
escalated quickly, and for the first time I could hear God giving
me very specific direction: "Be quiet, pack one bag, and leave."

And that's exactly what I did.

As soon as Martin left the room, I crammed whatever I could
get my hands on into one suitcase, grabbed our baby girl, took
a deep breath, and walked out.

"It's going to be okay, baby," I whispered in Jasmin's ear as
we left, even though I had no idea if that was true. I didn't want
to leave because I knew that no matter how much we fought,

there was still a bond between us, and that extended to our daughter. I was leaving so we could cool off—divorce wasn't on my mind at that time. I just knew I had to get out, and I walked out that door confident that leaving was the right decision for the moment. But I had little money. I had no plan. And I had no idea where we would go for the night.

I'm sure people thought that because I was married to a successful movie star I had a lot of resources. But because I loved him so much and wanted to be together, I gave up certain rights to marry him. I'd signed a prenuptial agreement, so when I left that night I had very little money or resources available to me.

Plus, all my family and support system, except for my sister, Pam, were back in Virginia, three thousand miles away. Here I was in the middle of the night driving around crying and wondering what I should do. Jasmin slept in her car seat; my suitcase slid around in the trunk. I couldn't go to Pam's apartment for fear that Martin could find me there. So I called my friend Sheree Smith, the former wife of Will Smith. We had bonded on the set of *Bad Boys*. She invited us to sleep over and welcomed us with open arms. In that moment, there was a hint of levity. Time away would give Martin and me space to think, plan, and recommit.

Even at that moment, I never expected our separation to be forever.

I didn't sleep at all that night. In the morning, as the sunlight poured in through the bedroom window, cold, ugly reality hit. I knew I couldn't go back, let alone allow my baby girl to grow up in an environment where her parents were always fighting. I was now without a husband or a home for myself and my daughter, and I had no credit cards or money. Most devastating, I was without any hope. After only eighteen months of marriage, everything was unraveling. My heart was aching. How had I failed so completely? What would the future be like for Jasmin? For me?

And the shame. What would everyone back in Virginia, who had such big hopes and dreams for me, think now? I didn't want to be a disappointment.

I hurt for my daddy, who had just lost his wife of thirty years, and now I knew I would be adding to his grief and stress. I didn't want him to know that his baby girl was homeless with a nine-month-old daughter, but I also didn't want to keep anything from him. I felt guilty and uncertain of what to do next. Eventually, I got an attorney, was awarded temporary support, and was able to move into a hotel.

That first Sunday after we left, I decided to take Jasmin to church. I went to the only church I knew of, a high-profile place of worship in the Hollywood community, and hoped I could sort of blend in with the rest of the congregation. But that didn't happen. With a friendly, welcoming heart, the pastor said from the pulpit, "I want to personally welcome Mrs. Martin Lawrence today."

Obviously, Pastor hadn't been keeping up with the tabloids. I wanted to crawl under the pew and wait for everyone to leave, but instead I faked a smile and gave a polite head nod. After service ended, I headed straight for the door, led by embarrassment and humiliation. Then I heard someone call my name. It was a friend I hadn't seen in a while. "Take care of you and your baby and stay focused on God, and I promise you everything is going to be all right."

My friend's words of encouragement were exactly what I needed to hear; I replayed her comments over and over and over as I worked to move forward. I tried desperately to establish a normal routine for Jasmin's sake. It was so difficult to do while living in a hotel. Plus, I was sad. Unbelievably sad.

As Jasmin slept, I watched her little tummy rise and fall peacefully. She had no idea she was stuck in a gray hotel crib with iron bars that looked like a prison cell. But I did. Where had her adorable pink fluffy curtains gone? Where was the beautiful carousel that was in her nursery? Where were her toys, stuffed animals, and baby pictures?

What had I done to her? To us? I still desperately loved Martin. How could I ever get through the mess?

I was running on empty. Pam had recently moved to L.A. and did everything she could to help me to my feet. She was the brilliant soul who suggested we find a church. After my last embarrassing encounter at a church, I was hesitant. But Pam knew what was missing: my personal relationship with the Lord. As I've said, I had always been a churchgoer, but I never took that all-important step of establishing my personal relationship with God. Pam had, and now she wanted me to come to know Him in a much more personal way. She was attending a church pastored by Bishop Noel Jones and encouraged me to go with her one Sunday. As we drove to Greater Bethany Community Church, I struggled to push my doubts down in light of my last experience.

The first Sunday we visited Bishop Jones's church, we slipped in and sat in the back. As he spoke about God's unconditional love and forgiveness, I hung on every word. It was the first time I had felt peace in a long time.

After service, we were introduced to Bishop Jones. He was so gracious and kind; my thirsty soul desperately needed God's comfort and His Word. The separation between Martin and I became permanent, and we were being beaten up in the tabloids about our "messy divorce." I had to grieve over the end of our marriage with the whole world watching. I felt ashamed and embarrassed that I wasn't able to make my marriage work. I felt guilty and sad that I had made Jasmin a child of divorce. And I felt very much alone. Bishop Jones and his church gave me a welcome place to recover. Soon after we joined, Bishop Jones's assistant, Marjorie Duncan, pulled me into a small, private room in the church and closed the curtain. "You can come here and worship with us any time you want," she said. "We got you."

Her words meant the world to me. I was so happy that someone understood and cared about my situation with no judgment or questions. I needed to heal. I needed a safe place to do that. I went to that wonderful church with Jasmin every Sunday and again on Wednesdays for Bible study. I learned so much about who God was, but more important, I was learning who God was *to me*.

I'd felt so broken, despondent, and terrified. I was in a city that never felt like home, and I was in the news, the tabloids, and the gossip mill. I had a baby daughter who needed a strong mommy, and I'd fallen apart.

I felt like a failure.

I slowly realized that up until this point in my life, at age twenty-six, I'd always gotten through everything with Christ. He was carrying me even when I didn't realize it. He showed me grace and mercy. But in the wake of my divorce, it certainly didn't feel like it. I couldn't see or feel anything except fear and anxiety. I was embarrassed.

But the church and the people and the Lord's Word lifted me up. After a nearly two-year absence from church, there I was, back in the house of the Lord. I was attending services regularly again. Bishop Jones and Marjorie and the entire congregation were so kind to me, the message so inspiring and powerful. Here, no one looked at me or whispered. There was just love. I was able to focus and work on my relationship with the Lord. And this love and understanding between God and me is exactly what prompted me to walk to the altar on a Wednesday and ask Jesus to be the Lord of my life. With tears streaming down my face, I gave my whole heart to God. I gave it to Him broken and empty, and He began putting it back together and filling it with His love. The more time I spent with God, the more empowered I felt. My circumstances hadn't changed. I was still a young single mother with a failed marriage in my past, but I finally had the courage to get back up and begin again. I was finally strong enough to believe that God had a plan for me, and I was learning to trust Him with my past, my present, and my future.

In that church on that particular day, I felt so comfortable and protected and loved that my spirit opened up. I confessed to all that Jesus Christ was my Savior.

The void was filled.

I was saved.

Set free.

And covered for all of my past sins.

This was the start of my second chance.

After the day I recommitted my life to God, I focused on studying the Word, truly understanding the meaning and message. While I'd always believed in and loved God, I didn't know the Bible. There are *four* Johns? I'd been intimidated, but now I welcomed the challenge of learning, and more important, I welcomed a relationship with God.

Leaving my marriage to Martin was terrifying. It killed me that I was being forced to uproot my daughter, turn over my life, and break up the family. I grew up believing that marriage was meant to last forever and that you stay together no matter the struggles. The people I looked up to most had done it. My grandparents were married for more than sixty years until my grandmother passed away. (My grandfather passed two weeks later, I believe at least in part due to the strong love they shared.) My parents were married for nearly thirty-one years. I watched my daddy tirelessly care for my mother until she lost her battle with breast cancer. When I married Martin, I truly meant it to be forever. It just didn't turn out that way.

I knew God was working on me, and I knew there was a journey that had now officially begun. A second chance changes everything. I learned that sometimes your path is revealed only when you have the vantage point to see where it is you need to go. Sometimes you must hit rock bottom before the view is clear. And you can only truly embrace that second chance when you're open to it, when you want it, and when you let God help you.

When this happens, you're ready to move on, with the Lord by your side. You're ready to make the most of your second chance. For me, that second chance included a new marriage, being a mommy again and again and again, and living a life filled with blessings and wonder. And now we enjoy an even closer and healthier relationship with Martin, his precious daughters and their mom, Shamicka, and a beautiful reconciliation with his family whom I loved and love even more now.

I couldn't accomplish the goals He had for me without letting Him guide me. You have to be in a place where you know in your heart and soul that God is everything. God puts people in your life as vessels for love and guidance, to help you grow, get direction, and gain confidence and strength. That's how you become unstuck.

And it's definitely how you have the wisdom, strength, and faith to harness your second chance.

Power Points

- Listen to God's voice when He speaks to you. God often speaks in little whispers, so pay attention.
- Be open to trying a new church and searching for the one that fits you.
- Don't be afraid or ashamed to ask for help.

Power Prompters

- When was there a moment in your life when you had a second-chance opportunity?
- Did you act on it, or did you miss it?
- Take a moment to reflect on the things that have gotten you stuck in life. Do you feel like you're stuck now?
- What steps will you take toward starting or strengthening your relationship with God?

Getting Back Up

Once you've been down and out, crawling around on the very bottom and praying for a way to restart and restore, once you've asked the Lord for help and grace and mercy, and once you truly understand that it is through Him that you are strong, you are in the best position to get back up.

It's impossible to capture in a couple of sentences the nuances and struggles each and every one of us has in the journey to move from despair to unstuck. But once you accept God's wisdom and understand that He is here to help, then you must take that power and actually begin piecing your life back together.

Is it easy? No.

But you can do it. No matter how many times you're beaten down, with faith and determination you can begin anew.

After I was saved, the next phase of my journey began. My life had shifted from married to unmarried, and with that came a whole bunch of loss, the least of which was my privacy and public image. I didn't want to share my personal grief with the world, but the media forced me to with every headline and photo. Rumors swirled—there was even gossip that I was dating Jamie Foxx. (I wasn't.) I didn't want anyone outside of my circle to know my business, but they did, thanks to tabloids and television.

How did a young woman who had a simple life with wonderful parents named Mildred and Henry get all caught up in this crazy L.A. story? Can you imagine seeing your photo next to some scandalous headline that the public believed was true? My feelings, my struggles, and even my personal evolution were exposed for the entire world to see. It was a hard place to be, especially for a person who cared a lot about what others thought.

I also had to deal with all of the insecurities that tagged along with brokenness and a failed marriage. Life with Martin was adventurous and filled with passion and excitement. Now it was filled with nights alone—just my baby and me. Filling the quiet can be so difficult.

Months after I left Martin, our divorce was final. By this time, hotel living was behind me, as Jasmin and I moved into our own home. I enrolled in acting classes, pursued TV hosting opportunities, got on fire for the Lord, and started a quest to regain my career. I focused my energies on my daughter, my Bible studies, and my work. I even had a talk show pilot underway. I was seeing a therapist named Candice who helped me take responsibility for the things I needed to and make sense of the things I had to let go. I completely recommend therapy for anyone. Candice helped me discover things about myself I couldn't see at the time. For example, after my divorce, I started dating someone, and in the short time we were together, Candice helped me see that I was going down an all-too-familiar path. I ended the relationship immediately. I regained my power (again) and moved on. Breaking patterns starts with seeing where they exist.

Day after day, my focus was on learning the lessons the Lord had for me so I could get to a place where I could stand tall and strong and happy. Little did I know that fourteen hundred miles away in Dallas, Texas, a man I had yet to meet was going through a breakup, too.

Turns out, as I worked to find a way to get back up and learn what God wanted for me, Emmitt Smith was doing the same. And we all know how that story turns out!

Once you welcome the Lord with an open, committed heart, He is the constant in the journey to repair your life. Stories of survival all have that pivotal moment when we decide to get back up. The stories that center on God's role are the most beautiful.

We all have disappointment and hard times. Each time, we have a choice to give in or get back up. When I met Tonya Stafford and learned about her past, I saw a woman who embodied strength and determination after decades of abuse and difficulty. Today, she is thriving and making a difference in the community for victims of domestic abuse and human trafficking. But it's been a long time coming.

Tonya grew up in the Dallas projects, and at just thirteen years old, she was raped and impregnated by a man her mother knew. Her mother sat idle as Tonya's belly grew, and did nothing to go after the man who had violated her daughter. As difficult as that is to absorb, what came next was even more horrific: Tonya's mother sold Tonya and the baby to the man for drug money. She was a victim of *familia trafficking*, a term that means a family member has sold a human being. Tonya said she left that day and didn't see her mother or siblings for years.

Tonya lived imprisoned for a decade, giving birth to three of the man's children by the time she was just seventeen. "I had to have sex all the time," she said.

Tonya attended school until ninth grade, at which point she had to drop out to take care of the growing brood. Throughout this time, and into her early twenties, she attended church. "But I didn't know God," she said. It wouldn't be until years later that she was in place to "be still" and receive the Lord's message.

"I was by myself and kept looking at these three kids and asked, 'What am I going to do?' One day, God said, 'You're going to make it.' In that stillness, in that place that was my rock bottom, where no one could pull me up, God told me I was going to be okay." That gave her the courage and wherewithal to leave her dire situation.

With help from her neighbor, Tonya hatched an escape plan. She sought a protective order—which got her captor out of the house so Tonya could move out—and she left.

He threatened to kill her, but the Dallas police had her back. They transported Tonya and the children to Irving, Texas, where she found safety in a women's shelter. She was twenty-four.

Tonya began extensive personal counseling. And she began to trust people. She entered into another relationship, but it failed because her torturous past infiltrated everything she did with a fierce power. "I didn't know how to receive anything," she says. "I ended up pregnant, and I didn't know what I was going to do at that point, either." Older didn't make her wiser.

After the birth of her fourth child, she says she heard God again. "God told me to work on me. Focus on my children." She moved into transitional housing, got a job as a cashier in a café, and rebuilt her life, day by day. From there, she worked as a public transportation bus driver and then, in 2001, she got licensed and started her own in-home daycare. She successfully ran it for ten years.

In the aftermath of her enslavement, Tonya found and lost faith several times. It wasn't until she attended a church called Sure Foundation that she was able to fully believe in the Lord. There, the pastor and his wife took Tonya's family under their wing to nurture, feed, and guide them. One Christmas, after

Tonya had already prepared her children for the fact that there'd be no presents under the tree, Tonya's life once again took a turn. The church adopted her family for the holiday.

"When they came and brought the kids gifts, I had so much stuff that I was giving it away. That's how blessed I was," Tonya said. "I believed then. I believed people still cared. That right there gave me so much hope and restored my faith. It restored everything."

Today, Tonya runs an organization called It's Going To Be Okay, a nonprofit dedicated to helping victims of forced prostitution and human trafficking. Among her goals is building a housing facility for victims. "When I was saved, it saved my children. It took someone helping me and believing in me," Tonya said. "I believe that when I save one, I save a generation."

Finding a way to leave the past behind and look into the future through God's eyes in order to get back up is exactly what Yukeba Davis chose to do.

Yukeba's mother was addicted to crack, so Yukeba was raised by her grandmother in the projects of New Orleans, a place where drugs, crime, and teen pregnancy were the norm. When Yukeba was seven, a family friend molested her. When she finally wrangled the courage to tell her grandmother what had happened, she was told never to visit that family friend again. That was it. After that day, her innocence was gone, and shame stepped in.

Yukeba moved on, as children will do. She found refuge in programs at Kingsley House and a social worker who took Yukeba under her wing.

"She prayed with us and encouraged us by telling us that where we lived did not define who we were," Yukeba said. She hung on the social worker's every word, and that encouragement and wisdom laid the foundation of faith it would take for Yukeba to go after the big dreams in her heart. While she did question her goals many times—how could a girl from the projects go to college when most of her family never even finished high school?—she didn't lose faith. And with the help of teachers at her high school, she did in fact go to college. Five years later, Yukeba graduated from Southern University with a bachelor's degree in business administration, then went on to earn a master's degree. But her success and joy were eclipsed shortly after by Hurricane Katrina.

Yukeba evacuated New Orleans with exactly three pairs of pants, two shirts, one pair of shoes, and six pairs of underwear. She arrived at her hotel room in Lake Charles, Louisiana, a temporary home she'd share with twenty others for five days. While the conditions were nowhere near ideal, Yukeba had survived. That was worth everything.

Yukeba and one of her friends who'd also fled New Orleans traveled to Dallas, where the community embraced Hurricane Katrina victims. Dozens of churches assigned "big sisters" and "big brothers" to aid displaced hurricane victims. The First United Methodist Church gave them food, furniture, and clothing. Even better, it gave Yukeba strong female role models and mentors. Just like before, God placed godly women in her life at just the right time.

One of Yukeba's mentors was Sarah Palisi Chapin, who is actually a good friend of mine. Sarah later connected Yukeba to yet another great mentor, Fritzi Woods, who was then the president and CEO of PrimeSource Foodservice Equipment. Yukeba was hired at PrimeSource and got promoted four times during her tenure, building her résumé and her confidence.

Since then, Fritzi has passed away, but her legacy as a well-known, respected, and beloved businesswoman lives on. I adored her and considered her an angel. For Yukeba, connecting with

Fritzi, Sarah, and other wonderful, successful women opened the door for her career.

Yukeba stayed in Dallas and built a wonderful life, getting back up each time life's circumstances knocked her down. She gives back to the community who welcomed her so many years ago by working with Meals on Wheels and the Big Brothers/Big Sisters program, hoping to inspire young women the same way she has been inspired by her mentors.

"I may not have been born with a first chance," she said, "but instead of becoming another statistic, I found my second chance. My story is proof that it does not matter how many times life knocks you down—it's how many times you get back up that counts."

———————

When I first heard Bennie Brown's story of triumph over tragedy, I wanted to give her a big hug and thank her for getting back up and continuing to make a difference. It so touched my heart and inspired me that I had to share it with you.

What began as a normal kind of day turned tragic with one phone call. Bennie's youngest son, Broderick, who was fourteen, had been in a horrific car accident. His situation was critical.

"If your son does survive," the doctor told Bennie, "he will be a vegetable."

Those words pierced Bennie's heart, bringing her to her knees. She had a very distinct conversation with God that day, begging Him to let her son live. She didn't necessarily get the answer she desired, but she did hear from God.

"His answer back to me was, 'Hope beyond hope.' That is when I knew I had to fight for my son and never give up on him or God—no matter what the doctor's report stated."

Broderick's injuries left him paralyzed, suffering from a traumatic brain injury, and ventilator dependent. He would need

33

twenty-four-hour care. Bennie knew she would need to be with her son around the clock, so she looked into her options. God made a way where there seemed to be no way: Her company offered executives early retirement.

"I took the early retirement," she explained. "God's provisions are timely and perfect."

Though financially they would be fine, the sense of loss was great.

"I wanted to die. Not take my life; I just wanted to give my life for his life—trade places with him. At the age of fourteen, his life had not begun," she said.

But Bennie knew she couldn't allow those kinds of thoughts to overtake her. "I realized the necessity of being strong-willed and maintaining an attitude of never giving up."

In the early days following Broderick's accident, he was completely immobile. Bennie had to be his eyes, his ears, and his voice. She had to advocate for his every need.

After many months in CCU and ICU, Broderick was stabilized enough to be released to a rehabilitation hospital, where he spent two months undergoing rehab. His prognosis wasn't good, and Bennie knew that her son might always remain bedridden, wheelchair-bound, and/or cognitively impaired. But she also knew that God would have the final say.

Worry plagued Bennie. What would happen when Broderick would eventually be able to come home? How could Bennie care for him?

God made a way for her son to have everything he needed.

A month after arriving home, Broderick gained consciousness and recognized familiar things. Amazingly, he regained his cognitive state of mind, blinking when asked questions. He began home tutoring through the school, and eventually he was even able to attend school twice a week to continue social interaction in a classroom setting.

Over time, Bennie realized two things. First, it would be a lifelong recovery for her son. Second, her child might not ever be returned to her completely whole as she once knew him. Accepting those truths was key in Bennie's ability to get back up and live again.

"My life had been put on hold for so long while I coped with such staggering changes, I gave myself permission to start moving forward, to re-start my daily routines, including even recreational activities," she shared, even finding time to help others through her foundation, Hope Beyond Hope, which provides meals and school supplies to children in underserved areas of Dallas. In addition, Bennie has established a home health care agency, BLE Health Services, LLC.

Bennie has learned to mourn her old life while moving on and embracing new challenges and changes. "Although this is not the life I would have chosen for him or myself," she said, "God has a higher purpose and plan for both of us."

When you consider the strength, courage, tenacity, and faith it took for Tonya, Yukeba, and Bennie to move forward, you probably feel as inspired as I do. Tonya's enslavement didn't break her, and today she's dedicated to helping others break free. Yukeba's difficult upbringing and abusive past didn't stop her from achieving her educational and vocational dreams. And Bennie's journey of faith—advocating for her son and standing in the gap for his very life when the doctors had all but written him off—what a testimony! No matter what life handed her, she got back up, kept her focus on God, and never settled for less than the best where her son's care and rehabilitation were concerned. That's how we mommies are, right? We will do whatever we have to do for our kids. And remember: God will do whatever He has to do for you because you're His child!

Did you ever think of it that way?

He will fight for you.

He will protect you.

He will bless you.

He will make a way for you.

He will pick you back up and carry you if that's what it takes because He isn't about to let you get down and stay down.

We serve a get-back-up kind of God. He may allow you to go through some difficult situations, but He won't allow those situations to overtake you. He will be right there to pick you up and put you back on the path to your divine purpose. He can even take a mess and make it blessed. I am living proof of that statement.

You see, even though my marriage to Martin ended badly, that wasn't the end of the story. Because we share custody of our beautiful daughter, Jasmin, we have worked on our relationship for her sake. Over time, we moved from estranged to civil to wonderful friends to family.

Only God can make that happen. If you have an ex-spouse, you know *exactly* what I'm talking about.

I can honestly say I am grateful for my time with Martin. Not only did he give me the gift of my precious daughter Jasmin, but he also caused me to press into the things of God. I learned a lot about myself during those two years, and I learned a lot about God. I learned that not even the most wonderful people can fill voids; only God can. I grew up both emotionally and spiritually, which prepared me for the next phase of my life. So when I eventually met Emmitt Smith, I was able to give him my whole heart because God had restored me. I wasn't looking for a man to complete me because God had already done that when I made Him my Lord and Savior on that Wednesday night at Greater Bethany Community Church.

Maybe like me, Tonya, Yukeba, and Bennie, you have gone through times in your life when you felt knocked down by negative circumstances, or maybe you're down for the count right now. No matter the situation you find yourself in today, I'm here to tell you that it's time to get back up, dust yourself off, and begin again. Your past doesn't define you—it can actually strengthen you.

I was watching one of Joel Osteen's services on television, and this message resonated with me. He asked if anyone ever wondered why the rearview mirror in a vehicle is so much smaller than the windshield. He said it's because you don't spend most of your time driving backward—you spend more time moving forward.

Apply that same truth to your spiritual life. Stop spending all of your time looking in that tiny rearview mirror and start focusing on the road ahead. Move toward your future. Embrace your present circumstances and be excited about your future. God is there for every moment of the ride, and He knows your destination. Make Him your GPS.

God will use any situation to get you to Him. The ability to get back up is within you. Let the Lord help you stand tall.

Power Points

- Leave the past behind and look to the future through God's eyes.
- God will make a way where there seems to be no way.
- God's provisions are always timely and perfect.
- God will do whatever He has to do for you because you're His child!
- Your past doesn't define you.

Power Prompters

- Name a time when life's circumstances knocked you down.
- How did God help you get back up and move forward?

- Do you have trouble leaving the past in the past? If so, write down the one thing that continues to pull you down, and then tear that paper into pieces. Throw those pieces away as a sign that you're no longer going to be affected by that thing/incident/person.

- How can you help someone else "get back up" this week? Pray for a person who is struggling. Ask God to help you identify a person to help, as well as the best way to offer that help. He will.

THREE

Living and Loving Again

I needed to sit still. After all that had transpired over the past year, my focus was on my daughter and my career. Not men. I didn't want one, need one, or think about one.

Okay, maybe I did *think*. A little.

The new chapter in my life was finally taking shape and I was doing pretty well—at least that's what I thought. I was still sad, of course, and saw a therapist each week to help me deal and heal. When my BFF Tara suggested a trip to Aruba for Sinbad's (the comedian) Soul Music Festival, I didn't think I should go. It was too soon to be at such a public event after my divorce. But then I thought about it some more, talked to my sister and Auntie Cherron, and realized that getting away might be just the thing I needed to do. It would be a healthy escape to spend quality time with my Delta Sigma Theta Sorority sisters (or sorors, as we call each other). Fun and laughter with my girls—that's a recipe for healing.

I told my therapist about my plans and she was supportive of the trip, with one condition: "Do not give your number to anyone," she said.

We had talked about the importance of being alone so I could truly heal, reflect, and learn. So I made a commitment to her and myself that this trip was solely for girlfriend time. She knew my need to fill the gap left by my divorce after the near disaster of a short-term relationship I had right after my separation. (As I mentioned in the previous chapter, I ended it when I saw familiar red flags.) So we both had concerns about my going to Aruba. She didn't want me to rush into anything or make any mistakes—and neither did I.

I flew to Virginia so my family could watch Jasmin, and then I headed to Maryland to meet my girls so we could travel together to Aruba. We had a blast talking about the past, laughing, sharing, and just being together. One night we were out at a club and I ran into a friend, Terry, from my college days. He was now a pro-football player and was in Aruba vacationing with his friends. We had a catch-up conversation and then went our separate ways.

What I didn't know is that when Terry returned to the group, he told one of them about me. "I ran into my friend Pat, a girl I know from college. I want you to meet her."

The friend was Emmitt Smith.

The next night, the girls and I headed to a concert. We made our way into the arena and unexpectedly bumped into Terry—again! He was just as surprised as I was. He motioned me over to his friend.

"Emmitt, *this* is my girl Pat. Pat, this is Emmitt." With that, Terry just walked off . . . and left us standing there.

I know this sounds crazy, but I'd learn later that Emmitt actually noticed me earlier in the night. Even though we were in an arena with thousands of other people, Emmitt just happened to look over at the entrance and see me through the crowd. "I think I just saw my future wife," he said to himself.

So when Terry introduced us, it was Emmitt's turn to be surprised!

We exchanged hellos; Emmitt was sweet and charming. But I have to be honest. While Emmitt Smith is a handsome man, I was taken aback that night. His style wasn't quite like that of the guys I had dated in the past. Picture this: We were in Aruba. In May. So it was *hot*. And Emmitt had on a black leather vest, big diamond earrings, and a black Kangol hat tilted to the back. But when he smiled, there was a kindness and graciousness that I immediately felt. We ended up in a moment that I didn't expect—a special, sweet moment. I'd heard his name before, but because I wasn't a huge football fan, I didn't know much about him. But I liked him immediately.

As the concert got busier, we got separated. I rejoined my friends and didn't think about seeing him again. It was no big deal. Just a guy I met. A nice guy, but just a guy. Besides, I wasn't there for a man. I was there for my girlfriends. I'd made a commitment to my therapist and myself, and I intended to keep it.

After the show, my girls and I went to a club but had to wait in line to get in. There, again, was Terry, and when he saw us, he invited us to join him so we could get in faster. Once inside, we lost ourselves in the crowd and music. A guy asked me to dance, but in the middle of the song Terry approached me. "Emmitt is waiting to dance with you."

The song ended, I thanked the guy for the dance, and I proceeded to dance with Emmitt. He asked if I could hang.

"Can *you* hang?" I replied.

And it was *on*.

After a while, my girlfriends were ready to leave the club.

"No! You can't take her!" Emmitt begged them to let me stay. He assured my girlfriends that I was in good hands and even offered to give them his driver's license if they wanted it.

Now, we all know the last thing I should've been doing was staying behind with a guy I'd just met, but I didn't have a single worry. There was something about him that made me comfortable. He treated me so sweetly and with such respect. So I said good-bye to the girls and stayed behind with Emmitt.

We danced for hours! We were having so much fun, we actually closed the club down. I mean, lights-out, DJ-packing-up kind of shut down. We walked along the street from the club to the cab; Emmitt was so chivalrous by insisting I stay on the inside while he walked along the outside, closer to the street. At my hotel, there was a bench overlooking the beach, and we sat talking until the sun came up. He asked about all of the major things in my life: my daughter, my deceased mother, and my career.

"Where do you see yourself in the next ten years?" he asked. And then, "What would your mother think of you right now as a mom?"

It was wonderful. When I look back on it, I think he was interviewing me. For him to sit on a bench by the ocean on the island of Aruba and ask me such thought-provoking questions, I can see clearly now that this man wasn't looking for a booty call.

He was searching for his wife.

Meeting Emmitt on that trip was divinely orchestrated. It was just meant to be. From him seeing me across the arena to that deep, easy conversation . . . every moment was godly. "Whoso findeth a wife findeth a good thing," says Scripture (Proverbs 18:22 KJV). And after all of the years of chasing love, it wasn't until I took the time to relax and focus on myself and my daughter that this man found me.

The next day, my girls and I bumped into Emmitt and his boys on the beach. And just like the night before, we had a blast. In the evening, we met up again at a club, and since it was our last night in Aruba, Emmitt and I had to say our good-byes. He asked for my phone number so we could keep in touch. I remembered the promise I made to myself and my therapist. I told him I couldn't give him my number.

"Then can I give you mine?" Emmitt asked.

Ha! I said to myself. I promised I wouldn't give out *my* number, but no one said anything about not getting his. Emmitt picked up a flyer that had fallen onto the floor and tore off a corner. He wrote his cell phone number, home number, pager number, Cowboy's facility number, and his assistant's number.

Back in L.A. I couldn't stop thinking about Emmitt. I wanted to call but wasn't sure if I should. Would he remember me? How would he respond? I waited two days . . . and then I called. I could tell by his voice that he was happy to hear from me, and that made me happy, too. From that call forward, we've talked every day.

For weeks, we spent hours on the phone. Then he visited me in L.A., staying in a hotel nearby. We acted as friends. Our courtship was slow and steady, which was what I needed to be comfortable, and Emmitt respected that. At the airport before his flight back to Dallas he said, "I'll be patient." He kissed my cheek and left. A total gentleman.

We kept up that pace for a while, and then it was my turn to visit him. It was my first trip to Dallas, and I'd stayed up the entire night before with my girlfriend Valerie picking out all of my outfits and shoes. I remember getting off the plane and there he was, standing there smiling. I can even remember what he had on—dark brown slacks and a knit shirt. I was so excited to see him.

He drove me to his house, and he had a limo waiting out front to take us to dinner and to a Maxwell concert. Now, if you know Maxwell's music, you know it's sensual and seductive—what you'd call mood music. So let me set the scene again: limo, Italian dinner, and a Maxwell concert.

My man was definitely setting me up!

At dinner, Emmitt secretly told the waiter it was my birthday, and the band made a big to-do and sang "Happy Birthday." It was June. My birthday is in December. I loved the spontaneity of that moment. It'd been a long time since I'd experienced romance like this.

We rode around downtown Dallas, our heads out the sunroof, singing, dancing, and kissing. I was blown away by my first time in Dallas. In L.A., I had to be so careful, so concerned about the tabloids and people talking. In Dallas, no one knew me. I could relax and be free.

It was a perfect night. I felt adored and treasured and swept away. That's what Emmitt did for me. As a woman who was so hurt, I needed it. I thought I'd already had my chance at love, and I didn't know if anyone would ever love me again. Between the negative attention in the media and the fact that I had a child, those were two facts that could turn many men away. But Emmitt didn't care. When you have a connection, some of things you think you want or need go out the window.

That night, I fell in love with Emmitt. And I realized that God gave me a beautiful, wonderful, incredible second chance to love again.

Our relationship took on momentum quickly. Even though I wasn't totally healed from my broken marriage, I was swept off of my feet. Within six months we discussed marriage. Our families loved each other, Emmitt was wonderful with Jasmin, and I was the happiest I'd been in a long time. Everything seemed perfect.

Except nothing is perfect.

About a year into our relationship, I expected a proposal to be coming any time. At every holiday I waited for the question. Easter. My birthday. Christmas, New Year's. Even Grandparent's Day! But nothing happened. For me at that time, it was the ultimate exercise in patience! I believed God knew exactly what He was doing, so I just kept waiting. And waiting.

Emmitt and I planned a trip to the Virgin Islands with another couple we were good friends with. Before we met up, I flew to Virginia to be with my daddy, who was having back surgery. Emmitt called and his voice sounded funny. He said he had something to talk to me about. Was he going to propose over the phone? That seemed unlikely since we'd be together in a matter of hours . . . but maybe?

There wasn't a proposal. In actuality, it was the worst news that any woman in love would want to hear: His former girl-friend was pregnant . . . and the baby was his.

Never for a single moment during our courtship, not with all the women wanting his attention or the miles between Dallas and L.A., did I ever worry about Emmitt cheating on me. I was never jealous, never insecure. And I never saw it coming. He was my knight in shining armor.

I asked a million questions—who, when, why? How in the world did this happen? Wasn't I good enough? Was it something I did? What did she have that I didn't? The questions were swirling through my mind. I hated how I felt. I was confused, hurt, angry, and crying like someone had died. The person I thought he was had died. It was a death of the image I had for him. I put Emmitt on a pedestal. I saw him as perfect. I got so caught up in the rapture.

And now I was devastated.

Even if I did forgive him, there was another woman's baby involved now. It was all too much. I felt anxious and scared. I just didn't think I could handle it. I told Emmitt it was over.

But Emmitt didn't give up. He asked me to stick to the plan to meet him and our friends in the Virgin Islands so we could spend time together, process it together, and, he said, work things out. Emmitt can be persuasive. After much prayer and soul searching, I decided to go.

Once we were together, we spent countless hours talking. I needed to know how this happened. Did he really love me? I needed to vent to him and share how much he hurt me. I needed to know if this was real for him and if he was willing to put in the work and commitment to make it last. Even our friends intervened to help. While Emmitt and his friend's wife hung out playing cards, his friend took me on an hour-long walk. He was candid and fair, and the conversation helped me a lot.

While it took me years to fully forgive Emmitt (I'll explain more later), I eventually decided that we loved each other enough to fight for our relationship. Through prayer, God's guidance, family support, and counseling, we made the commitment to make it work. Emmitt promised me he'd do everything to be a great father, and that he would make sure I knew that he was committed to me and no other woman. We could do this. If we put our trust in the Lord, we could heal and get through this together.

Everyone in the family who knew how difficult the situation was for me and Emmitt was present when I met Rheagen, his baby daughter, for the first time. Emmitt had gone to pick her up, and we all waited in the kitchen. It was tense, and I could feel everyone looking at me. I knew they were wondering, *Is she going to run out of the house? Pass out? Freak out? Cry?* I didn't even know how I was going to respond. When the moment came, accepting this precious baby—the situation I agonized over and prayed about—took exactly one second. Emmitt walked into the kitchen and placed Rheagen on my lap. She was beautiful, swaddled in her pink blanket. She looked up at me and smiled, as if to say, "Everything's going to be all right."

I immediately fell in love with her.

Emmitt and I maneuvered the challenge day by day. I was still living in L.A. and he was in Dallas, and we were visiting each other as often as we could. I was at a crossroads. My career was starting to take off, and I was booking acting jobs. I was even up for a role on the daytime soap *All My Children*. But my heart was in Dallas with the man I was in love with. I needed to know what he wanted. I figured that if I was going to go through all of the emotions and difficulty of the situation, I needed to be sure about our future and whether or not I'd be moving to Dallas. I didn't want him to feel any sort of pressure to marry me, but I did need to know his intentions. He assured me he did want to get married, but I wanted to know when and where.

He wouldn't give me a straight answer.

What I didn't know was that Emmitt was working behind the scenes to surprise me at his thirtieth birthday party. I flew to Dallas, thinking we were going to celebrate him . . . and there, in the middle of this incredible party, he calmed the crowd, got down on one knee, and asked me to marry him.

It was one of the most unexpected, exciting, and blissful surprises of my life! I basked in the glory and joy of our engagement. I was on cloud nine.

We may have gotten interrupted, but we were on the path again.

Emmitt and I began our wedding plans. A couple months before the wedding, we traveled to the Pro Bowl. There, the chaplain for the Minnesota Vikings asked to have a word with us. We had never met with him before, so it was a welcomed moment. The chaplain revealed that God had spoken to him and requested he advise us "to consecrate yourselves in all ways." He went on to explain that we should abstain from anything considered ungodly and stay pure. He said if we stayed obedient to God, we would be able to successfully handle the upcoming turmoil, and when we stood before Him on our wedding day, we would feel no struggle or conflict. We would only feel God's glory shining upon us in that moment.

Emmitt and I both received the message and absolutely obeyed the instructions. When we returned home, we experienced many attacks from the Enemy, some of which were extremely challenging, but we held strong to the pastor's words and direction, and we made it through.

Our wedding took place at the Fairmont Hotel in Dallas. As with most weddings, there was drama and conflict, but it didn't matter. As I stood in the beautiful bridal suite getting ready to commit myself to the man I loved with all of my heart, I had a sense of peace that calmed my spirit. I never cried a single tear. As we exchanged our vows, there was a light around us. Just like the chaplain had promised.

The glory of God covered and protected us.

Has married life been without obstacles and challenges? No. First of all, I had to learn that no one is perfect and that we all make mistakes. Second, I had to take Emmitt off of the pedestal that I'd put him on. As amazing as he is, he's not God. It was unfair to make him live up to that standard.

I made a commitment when I married my husband to honor God and love him and our daughters. Every day I make sure to thank God and ask Him to bring us closer to Him and closer as a family. Blending a family is not always easy, especially under our circumstances, but I made a commitment and I stick to it every day. Do I get weary sometimes? Of course! But I'm so grateful to God for my second chance, and I rejoice in it every day.

When God gives us a second chance, it is up to us to decide how we want to handle things. A woman I met named Carla Wicks shows us all the beauty of perseverance and an unrelenting belief that God takes care of us so we can love again, no matter what life events unfold.

With four children in tow, Carla fled an abusive marriage and spent years struggling with poverty. She relied on food stamps and the grace of others to help provide for her family. When she was presented with an opportunity to interview for an entry-level administrative job, she grabbed it. That small step became a big opportunity for her decades-long career, and today she is a successful registered dental hygienist. But Carla will tell you the struggle with poverty and unemployment was overshadowed by one much deeper and more severe: the loss of her son, who was killed while on active military duty.

Carla describes this point in her life as the "pit of agony, a place that felt like a dark tomb." But despite all the sadness, hardship, and grief, she never blamed God for the struggles, a way of thinking that began when she was young. Carla said that while her childhood wasn't normal, she never, even as a kid, blamed God for her path. "This was a pivotal position for how I would cope with even more severe hardships I was yet to endure as a young, middle-age, and older adult."

Carla's son's death was followed by another difficult situation. Her stepdaughter gave birth to a drug-addicted premature baby, and she was unable to care for her. Carla realized she and her husband were the baby's best hope for a good future. That meant retirement would have to wait. They took the child in and hoped eventually the baby would be reunited with her mother. But they were the only ones who had the desire to provide for the child, and God made it clear that His choice for them was to adopt Nicole. Tragically, Carla's stepdaughter died, but the child was in good hands.

"From the depths of poverty I never thought possible and the unbearable grief of losing a child, to the overwhelming responsibility of parenting again, I determined, while in each rut, to make a positive difference and turn those events that could have destroyed me and my spirit into something I could help others maneuver," Carla shares. "I have been sustained in every trial by treasuring the gifts God has given me with a pure gratitude that is not circumstantial. I am thankful in the good times *and* the bad. The most precious blessings are my husband, children, and grandchildren."

Today, Carla's adopted daughter, Nicole, is a thriving preteen. Carla says that in the face of any difficulty, she does what she's done since she gave her life to the Lord in 1974. She asks Him to teach her what she needs to learn. "He is faithful to do it every time," she says. "You have to be willing to ask."

Another story I have to share belongs to Kay Walker Cotton. On June 25, 1966, Kay suffered a tragic double loss: Her mother passed away in the morning from breast cancer, and later in the day, her husband, Essic, was killed in a car accident. One day forever changed life for this young mother of three, and Kay was forced to do everything alone. Kay attended church regularly. She processed her tragedies by taking things one day at a time and focusing on work. Years later, Kay met another man who would become her second husband, and together they had a son. While Kay thought the marriage was forever, it ended in divorce. Once again, Kay struggled to move on, and once again she had the sole responsibility of taking care of her family.

In 1991, tragedy struck again. Kay's daughter, Latonia, died after more than two years battling a painful illness. "The loss of a child is something you can only overcome by the grace of God," she said. She dealt with the grief through continual prayer, daily visits to the cemetery, and a support group. Latonia left behind a three-year-old son, and Kay took custody of him. Eight years later, Kay found love again. On the exact day thirty-three years after her husband and mother had died, Kay got what she calls her "real second chance" when she married Ardis Cotton. The two have had a strong, loving marriage, and he has been by her side through her battle with multiple myeloma cancer, bone marrow transplants, the joy of remission, and then the recent devastating news that the cancer had returned. She says life over the past ten years has been a journey with her husband in living out Proverbs 3:5–6: "Trust in the Lord with all your heart and lean not on your own understanding; in all your ways submit to him, and he will make your paths straight."

Kay's life has been one of service to others. She's raised nephews and nieces, helped struggling women in the community, and taught Sunday school. She has taken her second chances and used her strength and love to give back to others.

When you consider all of the women, including Carla and Kay, who have been through gut-wrenching, life-threatening, emotionally devastating experiences, you must stop to think of how it is that they are able to get up every morning and move on.

One word: God.

Through the guidance and love of God, anything is possible. In each example—my story of finding love and marriage again with Emmitt; Carla's story of finding a motherly love again with her adopted daughter, Nicole; and Kay's story of finding marriage and partnership again with Ardis—you see the common theme: The dominant role that God plays in each of our lives. God gives us second chances so we can love and live again, and so that we can heal and be whole.

Our boundless belief in the Lord is what we must rely on to overcome, to celebrate, and to live life to the fullest. In order to love and live again, you have to let go of your past and embrace the possibilities of the future. You have to open your heart and allow God to heal the broken places.

And most important, we must all learn to love past our pain, hurt, and disappointment, as Christ loves us.

Power Points

- God gives us the opportunity to love and live again.
- God gives us the strength to move on.
- We can be grateful to God for our blessings and struggles, for we learn and grow from each one.

Power Prompters

- Describe a time when you found love again, whether that means a second spouse, another child, or even a new friend.
- How will you live life to the fullest? What is something you always wanted to do that has been made possible through a second chance?

FOUR
Experiencing Forgiveness

Rheagen was just a little girl when she showed us how serious she was about playing soccer. She was in an outdoor league through the YMCA, and her team lost a game. While the other kids shrugged the loss away to chase butterflies or run around, Rheagen had a full-on meltdown. She was crying—seriously hurt and mad that her team was defeated. This was the first time I'd ever seen a child that young know what she wanted to do long-term. I recognized that the way she was acting meant she really cared about the game. It was an incredible, special moment. And the fact that now she's playing soccer in high school and has already been offered scholarships to play for college is all the more poignant for me. I've had the privilege of seeing her on this journey from the beginning, and I've watched her mature and grow as an athlete and a young lady. I can't imagine missing any of those special moments with her.

But it could've come to that had I not been able to forgive Emmitt.

As I explained earlier, Emmitt and I had the difficult task of overcoming some serious issues in order to make our marriage work. Every day I had to focus on forgiveness and commit to overcoming my own insecurities and fears in order to be with the man I love so dearly. Had I not been committed to embracing those difficult situations as opportunities, I never would've witnessed Rheagen on the field that day. I would have never watched her grow up or experienced any of the joy and honor of being her bonus mommy. Had Emmitt and I not been able to work through the situation all those years ago, had I not tried to let go of my fears, I never would have had the opportunity to see this beautiful baby girl blossom into a confident, free-spirited, kind, hardworking young woman. Because of forgiveness, there have been so many special moments I've been a part of. I've been blessed to be on a journey with her.

Throughout my life, I've had to work hard to forgive many times. In each instance, the reward far exceeded the pain of getting there. Had Martin and I not overcome our issues, our lives would be vastly different, but we focused on our daughter and our work paid off. Today, Jasmin is a beautiful, caring, successful, and thriving college student. Her father and I are truly dear friends, and Jasmin has brought our families back together with a love and bond that's unexplainable.

Had Emmitt and I not worked through our issues, we wouldn't have EJ, Skylar, or Elijah. But I know Emmitt and I were meant for each other, and every tear was worth it. EJ—named after Emmitt—was born on his daddy's birthday. We know God was telling us something! EJ is hardworking, focused, and determined—just like his dad. Eight months later, we were blessed to find out we were going to be parents to Skylar. She's the rock of our family; we call her the CEO of the household. And then came our surprise blessing, Elijah, who's the cuddler, lover, and comic relief. We call him the common denominator.

Without a lot of forgiving going on full circle, the Smith family wouldn't be what it is today.

There will always be situations that have the potential to put us in a place where we build resentment. Or maybe we feel like we don't have a heart of forgiveness because of certain experiences. But I'm here to tell you that through the most difficult situations and challenges, God creates the most beautiful opportunities for grace, love, reconciliation, and restoring of relationships. As I look at all that my husband and I went through, it is because we tackled the challenges of forgiveness that we now have the beautiful blessings God intended for us. Now I can look back and count my bonus daughter as one of my greatest blessings.

It's amazing how God can take tragedies and turn them into opportunities. He has given us all a heart to love. He has given us grace, the will to endure, and the hope of a brighter future. And He's given us a second chance for renewed relationships.

Just think what would've happened if I'd given up eighteen years ago. I would have missed out on a wonderful life with a husband who's been dedicated and committed to me. We've had the opportunity to blend together five amazing children. I'm not saying that our family is perfect. What is perfect are God's love and grace, which sustain us during the difficult times.

Forgiveness has nothing to do with the other person. It's about you letting go with the help of God's grace, and truly moving forward.

Matthew 6:14–15 says, "For if you forgive other people when they sin against you, your heavenly Father will also forgive you. But if you do not forgive others their sins, your Father will not forgive your sins."

This Scripture has helped me remember over the years that I have to forgive, regardless of how anyone else has treated me or felt toward me. After all, we can only be accountable for our own actions and behaviors.

I've also learned that forgiveness is perpetual. You can't just say, "Today I forgive and I'm over it!" Oh, if it were only that easy. It's a continuous consultation with God, and it can take years for you to really feel your heart and head come to terms. When I needed help, I turned to my therapist, Dr. Candice Zwick; my spiritual mentor, Cathy Moffitt; and my dear friend Tammy Franklin. Cathy had been through the trials and tribulations of a blended family, so she understood. Together, we read Scripture and talked about forgiveness. Cathy always brings me to the Word of God. I turned to Tammy because I admire her so much. She and her husband, Kirk (a renowned gospel artist), have a blended family, and they handle the challenges beautifully. I asked her to lunch so I could learn from her success. She provided me with a safe place to talk. She edified my spirit with encouragement and love. There was no gossip or bad-mouthing about anyone. It was all pure of heart, and focused on helping me understand the importance of forgiveness. These women helped me tremendously.

I've learned that when we have anger and resentment, we are blocking our own blessings and joy. Anger and resentment will stop us from walking into the fullness of what God has for us. I want to encourage you to stay focused because forgiveness is possible. You can't wait for the other person to change. Forgiveness is about changing *your* mind and *your* heart. That can only come from God.

Forgiveness requires a renewal of the mind. Romans 12:2 says, "Do not be conformed to this world, but be transformed by the renewing of your mind, that you may prove what is that good and acceptable and perfect will of God" (NKJV).

Forgiveness starts with accepting the situation. It is enhanced by letting go of animosity and negativity, and living with grace in the moment. You get help along the journey through fellowship, people who edify your spirit, and your own resolve. Experiencing forgiveness is one of the greatest gifts given to us by God. We learn and grow when we forgive. We show empathy and a focus that is greater than our egos and ourselves. Experiencing forgiveness is freeing.

It just takes a while to get there.

I'm often amazed and humbled by the way people can forgive in situations that bring unimaginable pain and suffering. One such person who has found the strength and courage to forgive after a horrendous act is Shannon Anderson.

It was New Year's Eve in 2004, and Shannon had planned to spend the night at home with her boyfriend. But when he announced he was going to a house party, Shannon, an underage girl from a small town in Texas, made the choice to go, too. At the party, she knew no one but her boyfriend, who soon slipped off somewhere. She accepted a drink from a stranger . . . and the rest of the evening was a blank. In the morning, she woke up in an unfamiliar bed wearing unfamiliar clothes. She had no clue who had covered her body with permanent marker, left hand-shaped bruises on her rear end, and sexually assaulted her.

In the emergency room, Shannon learned that she had been given Rohypnol, a date rape drug. The police wanted names, but she didn't know anyone at the party except the man she thought she could trust. As a result, there were no charges filed.

Shannon went through years of depression. She blamed herself for going to the party, for drinking, for not having control. She believed that she caused her own situation. She experienced humiliation and darkness.

She prayed to God for guidance. Over time, Shannon wrote about her feelings, sharing them on social media. The support poured in. Eventually, Shannon sent her ex-boyfriend an email outlining her feelings. She never received a response, but the exercise helped her begin to forgive the one person she needed to forgive in order to fully heal: herself.

Shannon believes that the events that transpired on that New Year's Eve have led to where she is now—a place where she can help others who have been through a sexual assault. She volunteered at a rape crisis center and shares her story through speaking opportunities. And when she won the Ms. West Texas 2014 pageant, her experience and volunteer work became her platform.

"I always find it overwhelming when I dive into a project expecting to share my story and bless others, but God has a way of using others . . . blessing me tenfold," Shannon explains in an essay called "A Path to Forgiveness." "I just know He isn't finished with me yet."

God doesn't want us to be unhappy, depressed, or feel shame. He wants us to be the best we can be so we can live up to our brilliant potential. When we do, we honor Him. I'm so proud of the work Shannon is doing to help others, and I'm even more proud of the way she has learned to forgive herself and realize her own worth.

To truly forgive, you must realize that you *deserve* to be happy—and that you are worth the fight. Just as Shannon realized the enormity of her value, so did Jessica Garza.

Jessica is a domestic abuse survivor. I had the honor of meeting Jessica years back when she was selected as one of our Treasure You Retreat Scholarship recipients. Jessica is one of the sweetest, most precious, and most vulnerable people I know. She endured physical abuse, jealous rages, and emotional torment—all at the hand of her husband. His abuse was relentless, even during her pregnancy. As a result, Jessica miscarried the baby. In the wake of the terrible situation, with no emotional support from the man who caused her such pain, Jessica realized it was time to go.

She left her husband on March 12, 2012, seeking solace in a church called Hope Fellowship and a women's shelter called Hope's Door. "There my mind was enriched and I was comforted in realizing that I was not alone and it was not my fault," she says. "I began to use my voice that he so desperately tried to silence."

For months, Jessica diligently worked to recontextualize the hateful messages from her husband. She had to relearn her self-worth and find the strength to work so she could support herself. A year later, Jessica shared her testimony at the Texas State Capitol in Austin in an effort to help pass a bill on protective orders.

"It's amazing the plan God has for you, and when you give it all up to Him . . . it is even more amazing how He guides you," she says.

In 2013, Jessica attended a Treasure You retreat. During the pajama session, another attendee approached her. "Is there anything I can pray for you about?" the woman asked.

With that question, Jessica said she realized that although she'd moved on and forgiven her husband, she hadn't yet forgiven herself for staying with him, even after the loss of her baby.

"I realized in that moment that although I had shared my baby's testimony, I had never said her name out loud because deep down inside I felt I was unworthy of saying it," she explains. "I instantly broke down and asked her to pray for me to help me say her name. Then I yelled with all my might, 'Mercy Elle!'"

Forgiveness gives us the power to discover more, experience more, be more, and love more. That's the ultimate. For Shannon, self-forgiveness has allowed her to assist others with finding ways to overcome a sexual assault. And for Jessica, forgiveness has allowed her to move away from shame and fear to start anew.

No matter what the situation or story, it is forgiveness that provides a cleansing way for us to move on and experience our second chance. We must ask God to guide us so we can step away from pride and hurt, release the anger and pain, and fill our hearts and souls with goodness.

Once you can accomplish that, your life will be lighter and full of peace, and you can move on to live the life that the Lord has intended.

Power Points

- Anger can block your blessings, joy, and peace.
- Forgiveness is a continual process. It can take years to achieve.
- If we don't show forgiveness for others, God will not forgive us.
- Give the situation to God and allow Him to help you work through it.

Power Prompters

- How have you learned to forgive someone? What steps did you take? Share your story with another person so he or she may be inspired.
- Is there someone you need to forgive? Write your feelings down, with truth and honesty as your guide. Once that's accomplished, read it aloud. Then, if you're ready, send it to the person you are working to forgive. Remember, you must forgive them whether they respond or not.
- Talk with a safe person—counselor, friend, or mentor—who will edify you through the process of forgiveness.

FIVE

Finding Your Purpose

There's nothing like a true friend. We give each other our best, and sometimes our worst, but we know our friends are there to lift us up and push us along just when we need it the most. In fact, my belief in the power of girlfriends to help us change and grow is the foundation for Treasure You. But I should start from the beginning.

The seed to Treasure You was planted one day when I traveled to California to watch my husband play in the AT&T Pebble Beach National Pro-Am. That morning, I met Jackie Rice. Her husband was also playing in the tournament. We struck up a conversation, and that led to a story, and before I knew it, we walked, talked, laughed, and cried over those eighteen holes of golf. (If you know golf, you know we had *plenty* of time to go through a range of emotions!) Jackie and I just clicked. She shared some of her struggles and triumphs that afternoon, and those hours were precious to me. I took comfort in her words and wisdom and felt a kinship in her kindness. She, like me, had been through a lot, and she could relate to many of my experiences. I knew I'd made a friend for life. We hugged when we said good-bye, and I left a little lighter.

That, right there, is the unyielding power of a girlfriend.

Six months later, I was at another golf tournament, the American Century Championship in Tahoe, and my sister, Pam, came with me to support Emmitt. As we walked the course, I had an unexpected surprise: There was my newfound friend, Jackie. I was so excited to reconnect after our time at Pebble Beach. We hugged and had a quick catch-up and promised to get together soon.

As Jackie walked off, I turned to Pam. "I wish there was a way that women could come together and have those moments to encourage each other and love on each other—real, authentic conversation in a safe environment, like what I experienced with Jackie."

"That's what you need to do," Pam said.

"What?"

"You need to create events where women come together like that," she said. "It's a great idea, and I think it's really needed. You can do it."

But could I? I thought about the lives I could touch, the stories I could help unburden, the friendships that could blossom. Pam's words stayed with me. I love sisters. That's what we do for each other.

Throughout that day and the next, I kept rolling the idea around in my mind. Pam's enthusiasm got me excited, and as I thought about it, I defined what I wanted to do: start a women's retreat. I shared my vision with Emmitt, sure that he wouldn't get it. After all, it was a "girl thing." But he was all over it.

"Baby, that's a good idea. I think you should do it."

That, my friends, was the sentence I needed to hear to be totally convinced.

With Pam's encouragement and Emmitt's support, I started telling everyone about my vision for retreats where women would come together, be treasured, treasure themselves, and celebrate each other in a safe environment. I received positive feedback, so I knew the idea was a good one. But something was holding me back. I would get to the talking stage, and then stop. "Who's going to come and hear you?" the devil whispered. "You've been divorced. You didn't win Miss USA. Your television career hasn't gone anywhere. You're a loser."

The more I entertained those thoughts the devil placed in my mind, the more fear overtook my spirit. So rather than move forward with the vision, I got busy and let myself become preoccupied. My retreat idea got put on the back burner. By me.

A few weeks later, someone from ABC called out of the blue and invited Emmitt to join the cast of *Dancing with the Stars*. I was shocked. I thought they were calling for me. (Really!)

"You're not going to do it, are you?" I was sure I'd be a much better fit for that show. After all, I was the pageant girl. I was the dancer. I was the performer. Emmitt was the retired, record-breaking superstar athlete who now focused on his new real estate business. He already had his time in the limelight. Surely, it was my time.

"Yeah, baby, I think I'm going to do it," he said, explaining that it might be a good way to expand his brand. (Boy, was he right! By the end of the show, he had a whole new fan base who never even saw him play a day of football!)

With his mind made up, I had to reconcile the terms. Of course I'd support his every step, but I was nervous. He'd be traveling to L.A., gone for days, and spending long hours holding on to a beautiful woman. There had to be ground rules for me to feel comfortable, and I had to spell them out.

"Y'all are not friends," I said firmly, referring to his future dance partner, Cheryl Burke. "There won't be any lunch dates or late-night Starbucks runs. This is business. She is your business partner, okay?"

"Got it," he said, smiling.

Between that moment and the day he left, he assured me I was the only woman he'd be going on any dates with, and that travels to L.A. were solely to dance. So, Emmitt sambaed, rhumbaed, ballroom danced, and made his mark on TV, thrilling audiences and earning rave reviews. And he did it in the city that had been my home before I married him. I'm not going to lie. I had a difficult time throughout the *DWTS* season. I knew Emmitt would do well because that's just who he is. He's a champion at just about anything he tries, but I never dreamed he'd make it to the finals. Week after week, with my hair and makeup done, I was all glammed up to sit in the audience to cheer on my handsome husband—just as I had done during many football games. I smiled on the outside, but I was dying on the inside. Like many of us, I was wearing a mask. I felt like God had forgotten about me and my dreams. Once again, like so many times before, I felt insignificant.

I was drowning.

On the night of the *DWTS* finale, Emmitt and Cheryl were named the winners of Season 3. Cheryl and I had developed a dear friendship through the process. The audience cheered, the confetti fell, and I celebrated with my family, so proud of my husband and his partner. I barely had a chance to hug Emmitt before he and Cheryl were whisked away for publicity appearances. They were headed to New York City to do the morning talk shows, and I was headed home to Dallas with our four kids. Empty. Sad. Broken. I needed to hear from God.

I did.

We were at church at The Potter's House, and Bishop T.D. Jakes declared: "I don't know what God has told you to do, but whatever it is, you need to do it."

Those words struck my heart with such force that I thought I would drop. There may have been thousands of people in service that day, but I knew that word was for me. And I wasn't the only one who realized it. My girlfriend Donna Richardson and my spiritual mentor Cathy Moffitt ran up to me during the service. They gave strong hugs and encouragement and asked if I'd heard what I needed to hear.

I had.

The next day I got up with drive and determination. I had my direction from the Lord to move forward with my first retreat, and I was so excited. I called my girlfriend Millicent, who was an event planner. "Let's set a date for a retreat," I declared.

That retreat grew into Treasure You. Within a few days, we had a date, venue, and tentative plan.

The first Treasure You retreat took place in 2008. This inaugural event focused on treasuring women who are married to high-profile men. The reason was simple: This group of women didn't have a safe place to go and talk without fear it would affect their husbands and their perception in public and in the media. About twenty wonderful women attended the retreat, and I got the opportunity to treasure them with surprises and pampering. I loved it! There was a lot of testimony and sharing. Lives were changed and dreams were birthed. Healing took place and emotions were shared. And there was so much laughter! After this first successful event, I realized that we all need to be treasured. That's when I decided to make Treasure You an ongoing thing for all women everywhere.

With Treasure You, I began to find my purpose: To inspire broken people just like me who needed a second chance.

––––––––––

Finding your purpose sometimes takes a while, and that journey isn't always a direct route. Sometimes there are rest stops, breakdowns, U-turns, and detours, but God uses every part of that journey as preparation. That's certainly been the case in my life, and it's also proven true in my friend Michelle Irwin's life.

I've known Michelle for more than eighteen years because her sweet mom, Marge, was our family's administrative assistant for years. She has become "Aunt Marge," "Mama Marge," and "Ms. Marge" to us all. Michelle has also worked with us in various capacities over the past few years.

Honestly, I'm inspired just thinking about all that she's accomplished. After graduating college at Florida State, Michelle went to law school and eventually landed a job with a very prestigious law firm in D.C. But after working twelve-hour days in a small office with several other people and no windows, Michelle realized that while she loved studying the law, she did not love practicing it. She left that job after only nine months and took a job as a general manager for a golf academy in China.

Though quite successful in her new position with the golf academy, Michelle wasn't content. She wasn't passionate about her job. Michelle wanted to write. She couldn't wait to steal away moments each night and journal or write copy for her website.

When it came time to move the golf academy to another location in China, Michelle knew it was her now-or-never moment.

She moved back to the United States and took an administrative job that allowed her to have one day off a week and most evenings to write. She took writing workshops and classes, and she continued to hone her craft in secret.

"I remember talking to an editor in the publishing industry at a pretty prestigious publisher, and he asked me what I was working on," Michelle said. "I told him I was just interested in the publishing process. I couldn't voice that I wanted to be a writer; I couldn't tell him that I wanted to be published. I was too afraid."

But as she continued to work on her book and connect with other writers, Michelle gained more confidence and eventually went public with her dream of becoming a published writer. In June 2014, at age forty, Michelle published her first work of fiction, *Another New Life*. I couldn't be more proud of her.

"When I saw that first copy of my book," she said, "I felt lighter. I felt really proud. . . . To have that dream come true, that was big."

Michelle, whose pen name is Sydney Aaliyah Michelle, has now published six contemporary romance novels and been invited to submit stories in several romance-themed anthologies with some of the best new romance writers in the industry.

"I've always wanted to be able to touch people through my stories, but I am an introvert by nature, and the thought of speaking on stage really scared me. But with writing, I can evoke emotions through the page. . . . Writing is my purpose," she shared. "I know that now. It's my passion. It gives me energy. It keeps me up late. It's what I love."

Sometimes the devil comes to steal that joy from Michelle, telling her that she waited too long to realize her dream of publishing, but she has learned to put those thoughts out of her mind.

"Once in a while I'll start thinking, *I wish I'd started writing earlier*, but you can't think like that," she explained. "Law school. The golf academy. They were all part of my journey. And I've learned that you're never too old to fulfill your purpose."

God's timing is always perfect. You may think that God has forgotten about your dreams, but He hasn't. He put those dreams inside of you, so how could He forget them? Lyenise Veasley, a Dallas fashion designer, can definitely say "amen" to that.

Lyenise began sketching at an early age, using her art to escape the difficult reality of watching her father abuse her mother. The only time she felt powerful during her childhood was when she put pencil to paper . . . until her mother left her father, and they started a new life free from abuse.

Growing up with her siblings in a single-parent home, money was tight.

"We were often given secondhand clothes, and we were grateful for them," she shared. "But I think that's one of the reasons I was inspired to be a fashion designer."

Lyenise's mother was also an artist and her grandmother was a seamstress, so she had a lot of help as she sketched and constructed her senior prom dress.

"My prom dress was amazing," she shared. "I was so excited about how it turned out that I wanted to continue drawing and creating designs."

The desire was always there, but sometimes life gets in the way of our plans. Three kids and twenty years later, God shoved Lyenise out of her comfortable nest and into her purpose. She lost her job and her home, and was forced to look for new employment. But when God closes doors, He opens new doors with better opportunities.

"I thought it was the end of the world for my children and me, but God works in mysterious ways," she said. "I was blessed with a new job that provided the means for me to get started on my fashion line, Soula'—Art and Soul Wear."

Today, Lyenise has completed an associate degree in fashion design and gives God all the glory.

"I am doing what I always desired—designing apparel," she said. "It's so amazing how God never forgets your dreams and desires."

God is the dream giver, the author and finisher of our faith, and what He started in you, He will complete. It may take some of us, like me, a little longer to fight through our fears and insecurities to walk in our dreams and discover our divine purposes and destinies, but if we will seek Him first and follow His lead, it will happen.

Emmitt shared a very special Scripture with me—the same one his grandmother gave him before he left for college—and now that same Scripture keeps me grounded:

> Trust in the Lord with all your heart and lean not on your own understanding; in all your ways acknowledge him, and he will direct your path.
>
> Proverbs 3:5–6 NKJV

That's so powerful, isn't it? The God of the universe will direct your path. The God who knows the beginning from the end will direct your path. The God who wants the very best for you will direct your path. The God who placed that dream in your heart will direct your path. You don't have to worry if you get detoured on your journey. He's God. He knows exactly where you are and exactly how to keep you on the path to your divine purpose and destiny.

The first part of that verse says, "Trust in the Lord with all your heart." Each of us had to trust God when we were scared, and we had to trust God even when it didn't look like He was doing anything.

I had to trust God that if I stepped out and organized a Treasure You retreat, He would show up and cause others to show up, too. I had to trust Him in every bit of the planning because I had no idea what I was doing, only that I was called to do it.

Michelle had to trust God to provide for her as she left her high-paying job and pursued her dream of writing for publication. It's one thing to say, "Oh yes, where God guides, He provides," but it's a whole different story when you have to walk that out in real life. And Lyenise had to trust that God knew what He was doing when she lost her job and her home.

Sometimes God has to nudge us out of our comfortable lives so that we can learn to fly. And sometimes when we ignore the gentle nudging, He will give us a big push to make sure we get the message. Those are never my favorite times, but those free-falling, scary moments in life are all part of the journey.

Though everybody's journey is different, the devil's tactics are always the same. He's still using those same old tired lies: "You're too old. You're too young. You didn't really hear from God. You'll never accomplish your dream. God hasn't got a divine plan for you." But I'm here to tell you that you're not too old or too young! You did hear from God! You will accomplish your dream, and God does have a divine plan for your life!

Jeremiah 29:11 says, "'For I know the plans I have for you,' declares the Lord, 'plans to prosper you and not to harm you, plans to give you hope and a future.'"

You might want to commit that one to memory so the next time the devil plants those seeds of doubt in your mind, you can boldly say, "No, I'm not going to believe your lies because I know the Lord has a plan for me, to prosper me and not to harm me, to give me a hope and a future."

The purpose that God has for you is just for you—no one else can fulfill it but you. That's why we have to stop letting fear, doubts, insecurities, distractions, busyness, and circumstances keep us from our divine purposes. What if I hadn't set the date and hosted that first Treasure You event? Lives that were transformed at that first event and all of those that have followed wouldn't have been changed. What if Michelle hadn't answered the call to write that first book? The readers who were touched through those pages wouldn't have been touched. And what if Lyenise hadn't pursued her passion of fashion and art? Her testimony wouldn't be a testimony at all, and the women she has influenced through her creations wouldn't be inspired. It's not always about us, but who God wants to touch through our lives. We are vessels for His use. We deprive others from being blessed when we allow the Enemy to stop us from doing God's work.

We all have a job to do here on earth, but when we're working in our calling and fulfilling our purpose, those tasks won't seem like work at all. You'll be excited to get up and get at it every morning. You won't need an energy drink or coffee to get you through the day because you'll be energized just from following your passion. You won't have to eat burgers and banana splits to get happy (though a Whopper might not hurt!) because you'll have joy in your journey. By the way, these are all things I did when feeling empty.

There's such a feeling of contentment and satisfaction when you know that you are on the right path to finding your purpose, but I realize not every person reading this book may be there yet. I've had women tell me, "Pat, I don't know what I'm called to do. I don't know what my purpose is." Maybe you're thinking that same thing right now. The good news is that God knows, and He is more than willing to share that information with you. In fact, He's probably been trying to tell you for a very long time, but you've been too busy or too stubborn or too fearful to receive it.

If you've not yet found your purpose, pray this with me right now:

Father God, I want to walk in my divine purpose. I want to follow the plan that you have for my life, but I don't know what that is. So I am asking you right now to reveal my purpose to me. You say in your Word that we have not because we ask not, so I am asking. Reawaken those dreams you placed on the inside of me, Lord, and give me the courage to go after them. Thank you, God, for never giving up on me. I love you. In the mighty name of Jesus, Amen.

Power Points

- Finding your divine purpose sometimes takes a while, and the journey isn't always a direct route.
- Sometimes God has to nudge us out of our comfortable nests so that we can learn to fly.
- The purpose that God has for you is just for you—no one else can fulfill it but you.

Power Prompters

- Has there ever been a time in your life when you knew you had heard from God to do something major, but you ignored Him?
- If you answered yes, what was it, and why did you ignore God's leading?
- Are you willing to do whatever He prompts you to do now? If so, what's your plan?
- What's your first step to fulfilling your purpose? Write it down—and make it happen!

SIX

Submitting to God's Will

I was so pumped about Treasure You. I just knew this was my purpose, my path. I've always had a heart to help women, and now, right before my eyes, was the opportunity to realize my dream. With that whisper from God, I knew I had the passion, ability, and tenacity to grow Treasure You into something great. Something important. Something that would inspire, guide, and help women.

And, it turns out, I had a Treasure You advocate in the media.

Amy Vanderoef, who was then a host on the popular morning show *Good Morning Texas*, met me for lunch one day and expressed her desire to help me host a Treasure You segment on the show. I was thrilled! She pitched the idea to the station, coached me, and within a month our segment aired on the show. We featured inspiring women who had stories to tell about overcoming difficulties and struggles so they could continue to achieve greatness. It was magical. I started a Treasure You website with Lara Ashmore, who was then executive director of Pat & Emmitt Smith Charities. And with Millicent Finney, my dear friend and event planner, we began rolling with ideas:

Treasure You products, talk shows, and even a Treasure You tour bus. Our vision was to visit neighborhoods in our decked-out bus to talk with women who are struggling and give them inspiration—and some much-deserved pampering. We wanted to provide a real "Treasure You" experience.

With all of my newfound energy and inspiration, I made it a priority to hit the gym, and I got back in shape. After birthing three of our four babies, you can imagine that this mommy needed to engage in some serious sweat equity! Months of hard work, healthy food choices, and a focus on wellness and I had my body back. For the first time in quite a while, I liked what I saw when I looked in the mirror.

I. Was. Killing. It!

Times were glorious for Emmitt, too. He was up for the Pro Football Hall of Fame, so we headed to Miami to hear the announcement of the new class. We were so excited at how well our lives were moving along.

As we anxiously waited for the announcer to call out the names of the new inductees, Emmitt and I were in the waiting area with his mother and father, along with the Jones family (the owners of the Dallas Cowboys), and other former Cowboys. I could feel Emmitt's nervousness and excitement. We were all bursting with excitement and anticipation.

When the announcer read Emmitt's name, we all screamed and hugged and jumped around! He was going to be in the National Football League Hall of Fame! I was overflowing with pride for my husband. I knew all that he'd been through in his career, from the time he was a little boy playing sandlot football with his cousins . . . to all of the bumps and bruises, wins and losses . . . to having people think his career was over . . . to winning three Super Bowls. And now, here stood this beautiful man, healthy and whole, receiving the highest honor in the National Football League. My heart swelled with pride and love.

I will never forget how I felt in that moment. I was wearing this gorgeous coral fitted dress given to me by my dear friend Dawn Mellon (don't you love girlfriends with great style?), and I accented the dress with bronze stilettos. I felt like I had power in me. I felt healthy and strong, and it seemed that the beauty inside was radiating. I felt so much energy and an incredible gratitude to God for all of my blessings. I was in a good, healthy place. It was my time to rock it out with my career.

Once we were back in Dallas, I decided it was time to do the one other major thing I really wanted to improve my body and my confidence. Now, we all know that after having babies, our figures aren't what they used to be. Things move. They stretch. And sometimes they look completely different than they should. After having kids, my body definitely needed a boost, so I decided to have a breast augmentation. This was part of my total body transformation, and I was looking forward to accomplishing this goal. I visited my doctor and got the pre-op checkup and blood work. I couldn't wait to see the girls with a makeover!

A few days later we would be attending our next sports-related event, this time the NBA All-Star Game. I wanted to look my best, so I headed to the Grand Spa in Dallas for some beauty maintenance. On this particular day, there was no kid drama, the birds were chirping, the sun was shining, and there were no backpacks, lunches, or uniforms left behind that had to be run to school. I got into the room and laid on the table as my esthetician, Michelle, applied hair-removing wax. Then the phone rang. It was the nurse from my doctor's office.

"Pat, we have your blood work results, and your hCG levels are high."

I have a history of breast cancer in my family, so my anxiety shot right up.

"What's that?" I was squeezing the phone.

"That means you tested positive for pregnancy," the nurse said. I literally jumped off of the table, wax dripping off my lips and eyebrows. It was impossible for me to be pregnant! Emmitt had had a vasectomy several months back. How could it be? The nurse had no idea what to say as I freaked out. She just listened and then offered the only advice she could: "Get a second opinion. Go get a test and see what it says, and give me a call back."

I immediately called Emmitt. How could this be happening? I had no room in my life to be pregnant. And the vasectomy! There was no chance! Right?

I stopped at the drugstore for a test, drove home, and ran to the bathroom. Two minutes later: positive. I showed the stick to Emmitt. He started to cry. Happy tears, of course. Mine weren't far behind. We hugged and hugged. There were plenty of jokes about whose baby it was, but I'd soon learn that with a vasectomy, there's always a chance of pregnancy. A 3 percent chance, to be exact.

And our soon-to-be baby boy, Elijah, was that little engine that could.

I'd be lying if I told you that I wasn't conflicted about the pregnancy. We didn't plan on having another child. I thought those sleepless nights were behind me. I'd given away the strollers, diaper bags, and car seats. And here I was, going on forty, and about to give birth to my fourth child. I questioned God. I thought it was my time to get my career on track and finally put some of my dreams and aspirations first. Another baby would derail my goals, postponing them for years. I felt angry and sad.

On the other hand, I also I felt excitement. But then the other side would creep back in. What about my TV career? And all of that hard work in the gym? But yet I *wanted* this sweet baby.

Both sides were fighting each other. I felt like I was splitting in two. Over time, the two sides would stop hashing it out and I, right alongside Emmitt, would focus only on the wonder and blessing of another child. After all, it was God's will. I just had to submit to it.

The pregnancy was difficult from the start. I found out I was pregnant on a Thursday. By Saturday, morning sickness hit hard, and it stayed with me for months. At just sixteen weeks I started going into labor. The doctor prescribed medicine and I had to stay on bedrest for days on end. This energetic, excited, pumped-up woman had to hang out in bed, tucked in under the covers. It was miserable! Depression kicked in. And that emotional state coupled with nausea and bloating didn't make for a happy person. I lost all inspiration, motivation, and confidence. The phone stopped ringing. I couldn't do anything, so why would anyone call?

This was supposed to be an exciting time for me—and for Emmitt! Now I wasn't even sure if I could attend the Hall of Fame ceremony. It was dangerous for me and the baby to travel, but I really wanted to go. As a compromise, my wonderful OB/GYN, Dr. Ezell Autrey, offered to come along just in case.

I was so glad to be able to participate and rejoice in Emmitt's success; it was an honor to watch the man I love fulfill his childhood dream. There was an after-party but my experience was much more chill than I would've preferred. I couldn't party or socialize. I had to sit down the entire time. I wasn't exactly the life of the party. Those who know me know I love to dance and socialize, especially with my favorite people—my family and friends. On this night, everyone was together in the same city, which hadn't happened since our wedding. And there I was, forced to sit still. It was brutal!

Even with all of the excitement and celebration over Emmitt's incredible accomplishment, the blues were never far away. I couldn't shake my depression. Self-pity took hold. I was low. And as big as a house! I couldn't exercise or run around, so that made me sad, and being forced to stay still is not in my DNA. My Uncle Allen used to call me "two minutes" because that's as long as I could stay still. One day, unexpectedly, all of these ugly feelings came to a head. The heaviness and grayness and burden had become too much. I reached a point where I realized I couldn't continue setting myself up with all of these expectations and then fall so far down when they didn't happen. I couldn't make sense of things, and I wanted to stop trying.

"God, whatever it is you're doing, for whatever reason, I just give myself to you. I submit. Whatever your will is," I sobbed, "my life is your work."

Right then and there was the moment when I fully and wholeheartedly submitted myself to God's will. Something inside me just changed. I realized that I had been chasing dreams, reaching out to do something important and be something important. I wanted to leave behind a legacy that included something significant. I'd always had a drive, but I realized that I was misaligned in my thinking. I believed that in order to reach greatness, I had to do it in a certain way. I never discussed His plans for me. Now I saw why I was running but standing still . . . and why I'd never catch what I was chasing: I hadn't let Him lead the way.

When I tell you how different I felt once I declared my submission, I mean that I was no longer depressed. No longer agitated or anxious or angry. I felt relief and confident that going forward, I'd have direction. Everything that had happened up until that moment in my life, when my eyes and heart opened so I could submit to God's will, had been for a purpose. There came a warm feeling of peace.

The rest of the pregnancy was still hard, and I struggled. But in the end, Elijah, my determined little baby boy, was born tiny but perfect. The moment he came into this world, I cried and thanked God for giving me a healthy baby. And I've never looked back.

Taking care of my new, precious baby boy took all of my energy and focus. For months, I had to sideline the gym, Treasure You, and what had become my normal routine. I struggled with high blood pressure and postpartum depression, which I'd never experienced before, even after giving birth to three other children. To compound my blues, for the first time ever, I had to stop nursing because of complications, and the mommy guilt was intense because I felt I was somehow cheating my son. The sleepless nights led to exhaustion (a state all mommies know very well), and when I could sleep, I often had nightmares. During this time, I was still trying to be a good wife and mommy to four kids.

Despite all of those challenges, when I had Elijah, I birthed something else, too. My attitude and the way I looked at my relationship with God had changed. I gave my life over to Him. I know that our inclination as human beings—and as strong, determined, ambitious women—is to control everything. We want to hold on to our dreams and desires and think we know what's best. Once I submitted to God's will, those fist-clenching ambitions just dissolved. It's not that I don't desire to do great things or have dreams . . . I will always have the ambition to grow, learn, and impact the lives of others. But now I'm much more patient and prayerful. I check in with God first, asking, "Is this what you want me to do?"

I put everything before Him. I ask Him who I need to work with and what I need to do. I actually bug Him a lot! I turn to Him for guidance and support, and when things get tough, I'm content in knowing it's His will. I'm constantly knocking at His door. But this is exactly the way He wants it to be.

While we may get a revelation from God, we still have to work through the process. It's not like we get a moment and everything is all better. It's a process to move on from a break-through. I still struggle every day, and I have to remember to check with God on everything. Submitting to God's will is a complete renewing of your mind, and you have to practice and practice until it becomes your norm. In my life I welcome suffering and joyful times all the same. I see now that it's part of the process that God puts us through. And since I've submitted to God's will, I've had so many more opportunities on this side than I ever did on the other.

As soon as I could, I slowly got back into a self-improvement routine. I went to the gym again, eventually lost the baby weight, and took things day by day. It didn't happen overnight, but with God's guidance, some pretty great things started to happen. I was on a flight watching a DVD from a "Woman Thou Art Loosed" conference hosted by Bishop and First Lady Jakes when I heard Pastor Cheryl Brady say, "Don't give up on your dreams." This was another one of those moments when God spoke directly to me. I met up with my previous agent, Babette Perry, in L.A. and told her that I still had a desire to do television, and if she heard of any opportunities in Dallas to please let me know. Within a couple of weeks I heard about an opportunity to co-host a Dallas talk show. Once again, God was giving me a second chance at a television career, which I'd always wanted. And this opportunity in Dallas meant I didn't have to move to New York or L.A. Within two months, I was on live television every morning doing what I'd always dreamed of.

I believe when you realize that submitting to God's will is the key to discovering the new opportunities He wants to present to you, you're fulfilling your purpose. I can illustrate a perfect example of this by sharing the story of my BFF, Tara Jackson.

Tara and I met my freshman year in college at James Madison University. We were sorority sisters and became best friends, but it was obvious from the beginning of our relationship that we were opposites. Tara is quiet and introspective; I'm all in! She was the one who always wanted a family with several kids. I was the one who wanted a career and figured I'd think about the husband and family thing later.

And then, in my mid-twenties, I got married. Tara was my maid of honor. A year later I had my first child. Tara is Jasmin's godmother. Throughout this time, the irony wasn't lost on either of us. Tara was the one focused on her career while I changed diapers. Wasn't it supposed to be the other way around?

Even with her many career accomplishments, including a thriving, successful career in law, Tara was frustrated with the fact that God gave a life to her that she didn't want.

Her frustration grew as she remained single, even as I entered into my second marriage and had three more children. For our friendship to stay true, we had to be open and honest with feelings. We had several defining moments where we expressed our emotions—everything from support to jealousy. She was jealous of my family life; I was jealous of her freedom, ability to travel, and successful career.

Giving attention to our feelings only strengthened our bond. We had God to guide us through the frustrating times. For Tara, frustration meant disappointment that her life was focused on her career. For me, I had to accept that my career hadn't yet taken off.

Now here's where the story gets really interesting!

Right around the time that Tara made partner at her law firm, she felt a desire to move to Arizona. She'd been to the state several times to visit us—we lived there when Emmitt played for the Arizona Cardinals—and she loved the area. She said God talked to her over a period of time to ensure she felt comfortable making such a big decision. Tara was worried about telling her mother—she didn't want her mother to think she was going through a midlife crisis or chasing a man. Not surprisingly, her mother was very supportive.

"Normally I would have been very timid about explaining my reasoning, but I felt a sense of peace about my decision," Tara told me. "A peace you only feel when you are in the Lord's will. . . . A peace that surpasses all understanding. When you are operating in yourself, you tend to care a lot about what others think, versus when operating through grace, direction, and strength, you tend to feel more at peace."

Six months after she arrived in Arizona, Tara started looking for legal jobs. But something didn't feel quite right. She felt a pull toward seminary school, but she didn't tell anyone. Tara, being Tara, needed to be sure. "It's not that others have bad intentions," she said, "but it's more important to know God's intentions."

Well, God led her to Phoenix Seminary, and even though she was a student, she didn't have to worry about paying the bills. "For the first three years my income did not change because clients from the law firm were finally paying up on old bills. There were times I was upset that I didn't get paid from those clients at the time, but God was saving and orchestrating His plan for me to receive the money when I was really going to need it—which was during seminary."

Tara graduated in four years with high honors, and she even gave the commencement address. Soon after graduation, Tara's friend Angela Alsobrooks called. She was running for State's Attorney of Prince George County in Maryland, and if she won the race, she wanted Tara to work with her.

"I told her, 'No, girl—I'm going to minister for a living.'"

Tara and Angela stayed in contact for months, talking about the possible job opportunities. As we all know, friends can be very persuasive! So Tara asked God what He wanted her to do. "He told me to explore all of my options—and that is what I did. I applied and inquired about all opportunities. And then

Angela won State's Attorney, and it was clear to me to make the move."

Today, Tara is the Principal Deputy State's Attorney of Prince George County.

She credits her career success to relying on God's will as the guide. "God does it different for everyone," Tara said. "He shuts and opens doors."

Right after she settled in to her new job, another door opened. Can you guess? Tara fell in love and got married, and within eight months, she was pregnant with her first child. My BFF got her greatest desire fulfilled!

"The Lord is faithful, and not only does He come through, but He does it with grandiose style," Tara said to me. "We get stronger with each trial."

Isn't it interesting how we think we know our path, only to find out that there are plenty of diversions and side streets? Tara and I are both proof of what happens when you submit to God's will: Decisions are made with peace and confidence, and you can handle anything because you know that not only is there a bigger plan, but you have His guidance to get you there.

I don't know what God has in store, but I'm thankful He is giving me the chance to experience so many things. All of the pivotal moments in my life are coming together, and I see so clearly now things that I would have missed before.

This is what happens when you submit to God's will.

Power Points

- Reach for greatness—just discuss the way with God.
- God wants us to submit to His will so He can be our guide.
- Sometimes the things you think you want don't turn out to be what you need.

- While we may get a revelation from God, we still have to work through the process.
- We don't know what God has in store, but He always leads us to where we need to be.

Power Prompters

- How do you work through the process of learning to submit to God's will?
- Share the moment or the time in your life when you decided to submit to God's will. How has your life changed?
- Think of an instance when you asked God for direction regarding a particular opportunity or decision. What was the outcome?

SEVEN

Pushing Through the Pain

I loved the spotlight. I'd been a cheerleader, pageant contender, on-air TV personality, and even student government president in college, and I was perfectly comfortable in front of people in those scenarios. But somehow, after the breakdown of my first marriage and all of the setbacks, disappointments, criticism, and public scrutiny, I lost my confidence and self-esteem for some of the things I once felt comfortable with. Public speaking is one example. The kind of heated attention that public speaking commands—standing in front of people who listen, love, dislike, and otherwise have an opinion about every single word I said, what I chose to wear, and whether or not I was good enough—terrified me.

This realization that I was anxious about public speaking came to light in my late thirties. My Aunt Shirley asked me to speak at an event for Girls Inc. (formerly Girls Club) and share my story of how the organization affected me growing up. When I accepted the invitation, I felt so scared and anxious. My anxiety was amplified because I was going back home to speak for the first time in front of family and friends. There's something about speaking in front of people you know that brings more pressure.

"What's wrong with you?" my sister, Pam, asked.

"Something has happened to me over the years. I just get terrified when I get up and have to speak in front of people," I said.

"What are you talking about?" Pam looked shocked. She knew I thrived off of moments like this. *Normally.*

I worried I wasn't good enough.

Pam assured me I had nothing to be concerned about. While I wanted to believe my sister, I couldn't shake the worry, and that worry stuck around for years.

With the help of my spiritual mentor, Cathy Moffitt, my speech was typed in detail and I read it word for word to the audience. It wasn't the perfect way for me to share my story, but it was a start. I got through it, and they heard my voice through those written words. It's important for us all to start somewhere. For me, getting out in front of the home audience at Girls Inc. was a start. And I slowly made my way back.

As we know, God works in mysterious ways. Sometimes He pushes you out of your comfort zone and into a place where He can grow you and use you in a way you never thought possible. That is exactly what He did with me.

In 2011, I attended a Dallas Women of Faith event. I went to support my friend Brenda Warner, who was speaking at the event, but God had much more for me than I expected. Originally, I had only planned to stay for Brenda's session, but I got so caught up in the ministry and stories that I went from tears to laughter. I stayed all day. I loved it! Every speaker had a message that seemed to be aimed right at me. After the event, I went home refreshed and revved up. The next day, Brenda texted me. The Women of Faith organizers wanted my number. I was curious to know why.

We met soon after and they asked if I'd be interested in doing twelve events during the next tour. Yes, I had spoken in front of some smaller audiences, but Women of Faith?! This was huge! We're talking about thousands of people in the audience. Down deep, I felt called to it. I was excited, and I felt like I could share my testimony. Participating in the Dallas event had touched my spirit. While I was there, I wanted to be a part of it and imagined sharing my journey and giving back hope and inspiration. To do so would be such an honor! But then those negative thoughts took over. Again.

I'm not ready for this kind of speaking engagement.

I'm not good enough.

When the organizers wanted me to join the team, I felt so torn.

I wanted it.

But I was fearful.

I wondered whether I could balance all of my commitments—my husband, five babies, Treasure You responsibilities—*and* go on a twelve-event tour.

It wasn't long into my worry that God put up a Stop sign and reminded me that when He gives you an assignment, He will make provisions. I meditated on that truth. After consulting with my husband, family, close friends, and business consultant at the time, Hattie Hill, I agreed to do seven events. Thank goodness we settled on seven, because shortly after I accepted the engagements, Emmitt agreed to participate on *Dancing with the Stars All-Stars*, so we knew our lives would be chaotic. (More on that later!) However, we approached these new opportunities like we had in the past, and with devoted support, love, and trust in God, we knew we'd make it all work.

I was still unsure and anxious about whether I should've joined the Women of Faith tour. A part of me was really excited about the opportunity to speak into so many women's lives, but then the Enemy would taunt me.

"There is no way you can speak in front of that many people," he said. "Those speakers on the Women of Faith tour are professionals with books and products. What do you have to offer?" That Enemy taunted me like the Great Gazoo taunted Fred on *The Flintstones*. Remember that little annoying character? He would lead Fred down the wrong path, making him doubt himself and his decisions. Well, the "Great Gazoo" was whispering loud and clear into my ear during this season. The Enemy was trying to shut me down, and I was falling quickly. I kept doubting myself, doubting my worth, and doubting that I had anything of significance to say.

But my spiritual mentor, Cathy, was not about to watch me let the Enemy win. Cathy had ideas of what I could do to succeed on the tour, and she worked with me. We prayed together and talked things through. I practiced with her over and over again. She asked friends to be my audience so I could practice. I listened to their critiques.

Even though my speech was personal and from the heart, speaking in front of large groups of people took my anxiety to a whole new level. I was good in front of cameras, but the Women of Faith tour was taking me down a road I had never traveled. What if I forgot my words? What if I wasn't good enough? What if the audience didn't connect with me? There was no "cut!" in front of a live audience. I had to remind myself that God was leading the way and that I was charged with pressing on. I had to tell the "Great Gazoo" to shut up.

Just when I started to feel comfortable that I could rock this new challenge, there was a change. A big one. The people who hired me to speak at the Women of Faith events were leaving, and there was a new team in place. This team had *not* chosen me, and they wanted to know more about me before my first official event. They came to see me in action at the Power Lunch Series at Prestonwood Baptist Church in Dallas. Talk about being nervous!

With the speech that Cathy had helped me craft in hand, I began.

"Everyone, close your eyes. Imagine yourself being in a room filled with hundreds of people. Everyone is laughing and talking around you. But no one notices you. You're in the middle of the room, screaming out, but no one hears your voice. Now open your eyes. That was me. . . ."

I went on to deliver my message, "Finding Your Voice," and as I spoke that afternoon, I didn't have to read my speech. I didn't even look at my notes because the Holy Spirit took over and the words flowed out of me. After I'd finished, Barry Walsh, one of the representatives from Women of Faith, came up to me and said, "That was good! Other than adding a few more Scriptures, I wouldn't change a thing."

Relief washed over me. For the first time, I actually felt like I had found my voice. I was ready for anything. Or so I thought.

A few days later I found out all speakers on the Women of Faith tour were required to take part in a speakers' boot camp. "I got this!" I said.

But I *so* didn't have it.

Our boot camp took place at a Dallas hotel. The speakers gathered and, as I looked around the room, I immediately felt intimidated. Each person there was an expert with credentials and endorsements and books and products. I really didn't feel that I was qualified enough to be on the team.

Each woman gave her speech and then received feedback from a speaking coach. She offered positive words and encouragement, and her kindness made me feel more relaxed, even more self-assured. This wouldn't be so bad after all.

I was the last to speak. I stood, took my mark, and shared my message. I used the same speech I'd given at church—with the same passion and conviction, or so I thought. With my last sentence, I stood there, breathing heavily.

No one said a word.

How had my words been received? Did the audience like it? Did the coach feel moved?

The silence was still there.

My nervousness rose. Anxiety was creeping in. I looked at the faces in the room, searching for feedback. Something. Anything. But it didn't happen. No one said anything.

The speaking coach, who'd been so forward with her constructive criticism with everyone else, wasn't saying a word. Those seconds were agony. Was my speech *that* bad? Did I mess up to the point that no one could even fathom what to say? Was I a complete failure? I thought I was going to burst with worry.

Finally, the coach said a few sentences, which amounted to, "Thank you for your speech." There was no direction or criticism at all. I was confused.

I figured it meant I did a terrible job.

I thanked her, took a deep breath, faked a smile, and forced myself to keep it together. I felt completely humiliated.

We were instructed to go to our rooms, have lunch, and rework our speeches based on the comments we'd received. I couldn't get to my room fast enough. I would've sprinted, even in heels, if it wouldn't have drawn attention. I had no plans to rework anything. I planned to pack my belongings, head for the car, and never look back.

As I rushed to my room, my friend Brenda saw me in the hallway. I immediately started crying and told her my speech wasn't good. "I shouldn't be here," I told her, the tears streaming. But Brenda wasn't having it. She gently told me to get it together. "This is a new situation," she said, "and it's hard—but you can do it." We embraced and I fled to my room.

Inside, I had an ugly cry and called Cathy to tell her what happened.

"The coach was encouraging to every other speaker but me," I cried. "So I'm going home. I think I'm done here."

"No, you're not," Cathy corrected. "You are going to re-work your speech and I'm going to help you. You're going to have something to eat, wash your face, put your makeup back on, and go back in there and deliver it with passion. You are anointed. This isn't about you. This is about what God wants to do through you."

I knew Cathy was right, but I didn't want to do anything she'd suggested. I wanted to run home and grab a Whopper and a banana split on the way. I was humiliated. I felt defeated. And I was hurting.

But instead, I made the decision to push through the pain. I got something to eat, fixed my face, and reworked my words with Cathy's help and God's guidance. Together, we prayed.

When I returned to that conference room, I was ready to minister my message. Fueled by pain (because God will make sure your pain has a purpose), I shared my heart, and the anointing fell. I looked over at Lisa Harper, a Women of Faith tour veteran, who smiled back with pride. When I was finished, she said, "Girl, you're a preacher."

This time, the speaking coach didn't fill the air with silence. Instead, she smiled at me. "Great job," she said.

I breathed a sigh of relief and thanked God for intervening.

That day, I learned to trust God so that His voice speaks through me. This was not a performance; it was a ministry. That made all the difference. I also realized I wouldn't be going through those seven Women of Faith events alone. He would be right there with me, speaking through me. All I had to do was show up and be His vessel. God was giving me a second chance to use my voice for Him, and I was so thankful for the opportunity.

God had surrounded me with important midwives to help me push through the pain—Cathy with her tough love, Brenda

91

with her cheerleading spirit, and Lisa, who spoke a word into my life at just the right time. The owner of the company that conducted the training actually used my journey at the conclusion of the speakers' boot camp as a testimony of the process! That's crazy, right? Using me—the girl who had very few credentials, hardly any speaking experience, and absolutely no books or products—as a testimony! That's a miracle of God!

It's often said, "God doesn't call the equipped, but He equips the called."

Though my pain was real and the process was difficult, I cannot even imagine the kind of pain that Tiffani Davis must have endured when she was attacked in her own home by a serial rapist. When Tiffani shared her story with me, I was so moved by her determination to push through the pain and grab hold of her second chance that I simply had to share her testimony.

It was December 2001, and Tiffani had just moved into a new apartment in Dallas. After throwing away her last load of trash for the night, she returned to her apartment. As she shut the door behind her, a stranger hiding inside attacked her. She fought him with everything she had, but he was too strong. He forced her into a closet and raped her at knifepoint, then escaped through the front door.

"Praise God I lived to report the crime," she shared, reflecting on that horrible night. "I had to undergo a rape kit exam to collect DNA evidence."

For six years, her attacker remained on the loose, known in Dallas as "the front door serial rapist." Tiffani had a hard time even getting out of bed some days, afraid he might return to finish her off. Her home, her "safe place," no longer felt safe, and she wondered if it ever would again. Then, there was a break in the case. The authorities found her attacker and arrested him. DNA evidence proved that he had raped her and seven other women. He was finally behind bars and awaiting trial. Tiffani didn't know if she could face her attacker in court. She didn't know if she had the strength to relive that pain. Courageously, she testified against him and helped secure his conviction, standing up for herself, the other victims, and all the other women who might have become his next victims.

He is currently serving two life sentences and will not be eligible for parole until he is eighty-six years old. (He was convicted at age forty-two.)

Though her attacker was finally behind bars where he couldn't hurt her anymore, Tiffani didn't feel free. In fact, she felt like she was in her own type of prison—a prison where the bars were made of shame, guilt, low self-esteem, fear, and depression. In 2010, she reached out for help and went through six months of intense counseling through a local rape crisis center. By the end of her counseling, she felt free for the first time since that awful night.

Today, Tiffani is a new person with a new love for life. She married in 2011 and, two years later, she and her husband celebrated the birth of their daughter.

"I appreciate life and live it to the fullest," she said, adding that she is using her second chance at life to help others find their second chances. She works with the Texas congressional delegation to fully fund the federal grant programs for forensic DNA testing in order to convict criminals and keep them off the streets.

———

When I learned that Anita Guerrero's last name meant "warrior" in Spanish, I smiled because she's a warrior in every sense of the word. She battled obsessive compulsive disorder

(OCD) and won the fight! But like Tiffani and me, Anita didn't go into battle alone. In fact, once she let God fight her battles for her, she experienced victory and a life full of freedom and joy.

Anita's story of pushing through the pain began when she was in high school. That's when her OCD first began. Because of her odd behavior, her dad thought she was crazy. Her mom thought she was crazy. Even Anita thought she was crazy at times. OCD was destroying her life, and she had no idea how to stop it.

"There were days where it would get so bad that I would just sit on the floor with my head between my knees and bang myself on the head with my fists," she shared. "Maybe I thought I could put back whatever was loose in my head."

OCD completely took over her life, robbing her of jobs, friends, boyfriends, everything.

"I was in hell," she said. "I was in a constant state of guilt and shame. I remember sitting alone at home one day, staring at the wall after a long session of counting, my OCD screaming in my head. I wanted to die."

As if that weren't enough, Anita's mom was diagnosed with aggressive cancer that same year. She passed away when Anita was only nineteen, and Anita blamed herself.

"I thought her death was my fault for not counting something the correct number of times," she confessed. "I was a mess."

Life progressed, and so did Anita's illness. Though she fell in love, married, and had children, all of her happy moments were tainted with OCD. The summer of 2013 was especially difficult.

"I literally could not function. I cried all the time, and my husband would have to force me to get out of bed. I don't think I've ever prayed so hard, nor have I ever heard my husband plead with the Lord the way he did that summer," she said. "Yet the Lord was quiet most of the summer."

But just because the Lord was quiet didn't mean He wasn't working.

Though Anita fought on, reading books on OCD, going to counseling, adjusting her medication, making trips to the ER for extreme anxiety, she felt that OCD was winning. She wondered if she would ever have a normal family life. Then, one day she had that turnaround moment. Somehow she just knew it was her second chance.

"I had been fighting OCD my way," she confessed. "But I felt that I was at a point where it had to be all or nothing. Give it all to God or don't give Him anything. I gave up. I said, 'Okay, God, I'll do it your way.'"

Little by little, the anxiety lifted and eventually left. She started getting up in the mornings without the help of her husband, and even made coffee. It was a small step but a huge victory.

"Every day I would thank God for just being able to function," she shared. "Giving God control over the OCD allowed me to give Him control over everything. A lot of things changed after that. I don't do as much as I used to. I take more time to breathe and to rest. I take more time to read my Bible and be with the Lord. When the OCD tries to creep up, I still give it to God. God is awesome. He can do anything."

Anita believes that God has given her this second chance at a normal life so that she can lead the way for others who might be in the battle of their lives.

"My husband told me last year, in the midst of all this pain, 'Ask God what He wants you to learn from this. No Christian goes through a hardship like this without a purpose.' Here's what I've learned: OCD can't take your life; it has to convince you to do that. OCD can't take your heart; it just makes you believe it has. OCD can't take your God. No matter how strong it says it is, God is stronger. No matter how big it says it is, God is bigger. I told the Lord that I would tell anyone who would listen. It is all for His glory."

Aren't those amazing stories of triumph over pain? When I hosted the first Second Chances event with *Good Morning America*'s Robin Roberts, she said something that I'll never forget: "People don't care what you've accomplished. People don't want to hear from you until they know what you've overcome."

When she spoke those words, I remember thinking, "Yes! That's it!" That's why these stories of pushing through the pain are so powerful! It's one thing to say, "I know how you feel." It's another thing to say, "I actually know how you feel because I went through that same situation and God brought me out, and He will do the same for you."

There truly is a purpose for the pain. My pastor, Bishop T.D. Jakes, says, "You can't take pain out of the process." God told us in His Word to expect pain, expect trouble, expect tests (1 Peter 4:12). So I don't know why we're so surprised when pain, trouble, and tests come upon us. But here's the good news: We don't have to remain in the pain, because eventually our greatest test will become our greatest testimony. If I hadn't gone through the fire during that Women of Faith boot camp, I wouldn't have been ready to minister to the thousands of women in those seven meetings, and I certainly wouldn't have been ready for these Second Chance events that are just beginning. Though it was a painful process, God used that pain to fuel my purpose. And by going through it, I was able to finally find my voice in Him.

He did the same for Tiffani and Anita.

When Tiffani fights for more forensic DNA testing in order to convict criminals and keep them off the streets, she does so with great passion. The devil tried to silence her voice with fear and shame, but God took her through the pain and restored her voice. And when God restores something, He doesn't just give you back what you once had—He gives you back something even better. That's just the kind of God He is.

The devil tried to steal Anita's voice, too, but God took her through the pain of OCD and brought her out with a powerful testimony that she freely shares every time she gets the opportunity.

In light of these powerful stories, let me ask you this: What's your greatest test? What pain have you endured? Some of you may be right in the middle of the biggest battle of your life, but don't give up. Don't give in. Press on and press through. Remember, there is purpose for your pain. God didn't bring it, but He will use it, so treasure it all because He will use it all. You may be on a path you never dreamed you'd be on, but God knew. And when He takes you to where you're going—your divine destination—you're going to love it. For me, the journey was worth it because I've learned to appreciate the painful times. Every pothole. Every roadblock. Every detour and delay. They were all just a part of my journey, and now they're a part of my story. They're a part of my testimony!

So remember, push through the pain. It will all be worth it, I promise. And even better than that, God promises.

Power Points

- Sometimes God will push you out of your comfort zone and into a place where He can grow you and use you in a way you never thought possible.
- Just because the Lord is quiet doesn't mean He isn't working.
- There is a purpose for your pain.
- You can't take pain out of the process.
- Your greatest test will become your greatest testimony.

Power Prompters

- Have you ever gone through something very painful, and when you cried out to God, you felt as though He wasn't listening or didn't care? How did you get through it?
- Looking back on that painful journey, what piece of advice would you give yourself, knowing what you know now?
- What purpose have you found for the pain you've endured?

EIGHT

Discovering Strength in Loss

When Emmitt and I got married and began attending The Potter's House as a family, I was eager to get involved in the church and serve the community in some way, but I wasn't sure how God might use me. I made an appointment to meet with the first lady of the church, Serita Jakes—or Mom J, as I call her. After I shared my heart with her, she said something that totally changed my life.

"Your misery can become your ministry."

I wasn't sure what kind of ministry could ever come from my misery, but I knew that Mom J was right. She was always right.

For so many years, I thought I was dealing only with the disappointment and pain of a failed marriage. But there was more.

When my mom passed away on June 10, 1993, I was torn apart, but I put on a brave face, pretending to be okay. I didn't want others to feel sorry for me. Yet I was the only one in my circle of friends who had lost her mom, and I felt short-changed. At age twenty-two, without my mom, I often felt abandoned. I was angry and upset and sad about all of the future missed moments with her: the day she'd help me find my wedding dress, the day she'd watch me get married, the day she'd hold her grandbabies for the very first time. When I entered the hospital about to give birth to Jasmin, I imagined her standing beside the bed, after each contraction telling me it was going to be okay, telling me I was going to be a great mom.

The reality of her not being there hurt to the depth of my soul.

The best I can describe it is that I felt like I wasn't whole. For my entire life, I'd had this perfect structure with my mom and dad. With my mom gone, I didn't have her guidance. Anytime I met someone who asked, "So, tell me about your family," I would become uncomfortable. I didn't want to reveal to anyone that my mom had passed away. I felt like people thought I was broken, and I hated that feeling. I wanted my mom. I liked my life when the structure was there.

To protect my heart, I buried those feelings deep inside. For years, I blamed everything and every person for my hurt and pain. After my first week of the Women of Faith tour event, in August 2012, I realized that there was something still raw in my soul. Something was missing in my message, but I couldn't figure it out.

I attended a prayer group session at the home of my dear friend Melani Ismail. Something divine happened that day, and I had the clear realization that I was suffering because I had not truly dealt with my mom's death. When God brought it to the surface, I let go in front of my dear sisters with a cry and release that's hard to explain. But that moment brought forth a freedom that I had sought for almost twenty years. Since then, my spirit has been lighter, fuller, and happier. I don't know if it was finally accepting my mom's passing or fully receiving God's message, but that afternoon changed me—for the better. That's what God does for us.

In 2013, I was asked to be the chair for the Dallas Komen Race for the Cure. The day I officially began my role, I spoke before a group of my peers, colleagues, friends, and cancer survivors. As I delivered my speech, emotion overtook me. I explained that I lost my mom to breast cancer when I was only twenty-two, and with each word, I was unable to fight back the tears. It was the first time that I'd ever been that vulnerable in a speech. Yet, in my vulnerability, I felt empowered, and my resolve strengthened. As chair, I made a lot of speeches, particularly during Breast Cancer Awareness month (which is October). With each speech, I shared my experience with my mother's death. And every time I felt a little bit freer.

I was discovering strength through that loss, and as I shared my story, I was helping others do the same. In each audience, there were many who had lost loved ones to cancer. Others had lost their hair or their breasts. And some had lost hope after their cancer diagnosis. Together, we found strength in numbers. It was an amazing season for me, but I didn't realize how deeply it had impacted me until the following Mother's Day.

Ever since my mom's death, Mother's Day had been the dreaded holiday. Even as I became a mother, I didn't like to celebrate it. It was just too sad for me. I always felt cheated that my mommy had gone to heaven way too soon; the holiday served as a reminder of the greatest hurt of my life. But on Mother's Day 2014, that all changed.

Sitting at our kitchen table (me in my robe and bonnet), I looked at my handsome husband and my kids and had this overwhelming sense of gratitude. We laughed and ate . . . and laughed some more as they celebrated *me*. I realized that just because I had lost my mom didn't mean my kids should be denied experiences with theirs. On that day—almost twenty-one years after my mom's passing—I promised that I would be the best mom I could be every day, as long as I was on this earth. I vowed that I would empower them and teach them independence so that when the day came that I was gone, they would be strong, healthy, and whole individuals who could carry on without me just fine. It was my second chance at being the mom my children needed me to be every single day. Including Mother's Day.

Ever since that aha moment at Melani's house, I've been focused on being the mother my children need. My revelation was timed perfectly. Before Jasmin, my oldest child, headed off to college, I put my wisdom into practice. There was one day she called me several times, but I was in and out of business meetings all afternoon and couldn't answer the phone. When we finally connected later on, I apologized for not being able to pick up immediately. But I didn't stop there. "Here's the thing, baby girl. I'm not always going to be available to you. . . . But I know someone who is. God is on duty 24/7 and you have direct access to Him."

I wanted her to know that. I want all my children to know that. I wish I'd learned it sooner in life. It seems we're all growing up and growing stronger together. Mom J was right. My ministry was birthed out of my misery.

I recently headed to my hometown to speak at an event called Victorious 2015 hosted by my longtime friend April Woodard and her husband, Pastor Adrian Woodard, of Favor Nation Church. In the audience were my daddy, my godmother Aunt Mildred, my sister, Aunt Cherron and Uncle Malcom, and my teacher Sandy Hutchinson, who mentored me as I grew up. There were plenty of tears about my mom. But guess what? I had victory over the pain. And I did not cry. The next Sunday, my daddy and I went to services at Third Baptist Church, the church I grew up in. I sat in the same pew as I did when I was a little girl, and I remembered how I'd lay my head on my mommy's lap during the sermon. I remembered being a teenager and sitting in the balcony with my friends, eating candy and chewing gum . . . and how my mom, who was sitting on the other side of the balcony, would watch me and tap her lip. That tap meant hush and pay attention . . . and spit out that gum, now! That Sunday sitting next to my daddy, I didn't shed one tear. Whatever that empty place was that had mourned for my mom all those years was filled by God's grace. I am so happy and in a place now where I can think about my mommy with joy and great memories and not feel sadness or cry. This change is huge for me. To be able to focus on the happiness instead of the pain is a testament of discovering strength in loss.

I continue to speak about the loss of my mother and how God restored my hope and my voice. And I continue my work in the fight against breast cancer. My mother was a fighter, and I learned from the very best.

So what is your misery? Look there and you'll find the beginnings of your ministry. Your greatest test will become your greatest testimony. Your mess will become your message. And God will take your ashes and give you beauty in exchange (Isaiah 61:3). While these may sound like spiritual clichés, they are much more than that. I've lived them and I can tell you this: God will use every last bit of what you've gone through, and if you'll keep your heart right and trust Him through it, He won't just bring you through the pain, He will bring you out stronger than before.

That's what He did for Amy Munoz, a very special lady that we honored at our first Second Chances event in Dallas in January 2014. As a mother, her story is heartbreaking to me. But as I learned how God has given her a platform to encourage others on their difficult journeys, I knew her story had to be told here.

When Amy was only seven weeks pregnant, her husband, Alex, learned that he would be deployed to Afghanistan for most of 2013 and miss most of Amy's pregnancy. While this wasn't ideal, the couple had been through long deployments before; one of Amy's co-workers even joked, "Alex took the easy way out. I would choose Afghanistan over living with a pregnant woman, too."

As Amy's pregnancy advanced, she kept Alex aware of every detail and filled out the requisite paper work so he could be home in time for baby Kaitlyn's birth. When Amy and Alex arrived at the hospital for the scheduled C-section, their excitement quickly turned to nervousness. The OB nurse had a difficult time finding the baby's heartbeat during the pre-op check. Amy assured Alex that everything was okay and that their baby had been stubborn for most of her pregnancy. About twenty minutes later, Amy's doctor showed up and rolled the sonogram machine into their hospital room. In an instant, everything changed.

"The very first image I saw on the screen was of my daughter's four-chambered heart frozen still," Amy remembered. "I work in health care, so I immediately knew that something was terribly wrong."

Next, the doctor moved the probe from Kaitlyn's abdomen down to her leg area.

"I kept thinking, 'She's still looking, there's hope.' But to this day, I think she was steadying herself to tell me that Kaitlyn had passed."

At thirty-nine and a half weeks pregnant, Amy and Alex lost their baby, Kaitlyn Sophia Munoz.

"I was absolutely crushed," she shared. "Beyond consoling . . . these things just didn't happen. Especially to people like me who were hypervigilant about prenatal care and doing everything in my power to make sure that Kaitlyn had a safe and successful birth."

Amy soon learned that it happened a lot more than she had realized.

"I'm a numbers girl, and as I started reading literature on stillbirths, I found that more than a third of stillbirths are never explained," she said. "As expected, Kaitlyn's cause of death was/is a mystery. . . . According to my OB, everything about her was perfect. There were no gross anatomical defects, and through the autopsy, we found that she was healthy on a cellular level."

Amy's research revealed a startling statistic—1 in every 160 pregnancies in the United States ends in stillbirth. People Amy had known for years began sharing their stories of miscarriages and stillbirths—stories she had never heard before.

"You bond with people when you have experienced such a traumatic and instantaneous loss," Amy shared. "And one of the most comforting things for me during this time was hearing stories of loss and hope from those who had gone on to grow their families after a stillbirth."

Amy began to realize that her story might help others in the same way she had been helped, so she started writing a blog, *kaitlynlives.blogspot.com*, as a part of her grieving process.

"I wrote from a very genuine place," she explained, "not hiding the fact that I was/am incredibly broken by the loss of our daughter. I had so many hopes and dreams for that little girl. . . . My heart is still healing, and there will always be a hole that can never be filled from my daughter who is not with us on this earth."

Amy's blogs touched hearts around the world. Through that outreach, she started experiencing a strength in loss that only happens when God intervenes.

"I see the second chance, or opportunity for growth, because our story has resonated with so many people," Amy said. "We have gotten notes from people all across the world saying that Kaitlyn touched their lives. We had strangers ask to do fundraisers in her honor. I have a gut feeling that in the future, my blog will be turned into a book. I know there are good things that will come out of Kaitlyn's story."

Amy and Alex experienced a great loss—the greatest loss of their lives—but God has been with them every step of the way. And just under thirteen months after they lost Kaitlyn, Amy and Alex welcomed Kiera.

"She is the promise after the storm," Amy said. "She's the restoration of our family and the fulfillment of God's promise to me as a mother."

Today, Amy helps to give back through her involvement in a nonprofit organization called Hope Mommies, which was created to bring the hope of Christ to families who have experienced the loss of an infant.

"God doesn't put a desire in our hearts that He doesn't fulfill," Amy said. "Our desire is to be parents, and here we are. He's going to be faithful and do what He set out to do."

———

Elizabeth Savage is another brave woman who shares her story of unimaginable loss and the power of strength and hope through God.

Elizabeth and her high school boyfriend didn't have a smooth relationship, and things went from bad to worse when she became pregnant. The verbal abuse she had suffered during her first pregnancy turned into physical abuse when she became pregnant with their second baby. For four years, she endured the torment.

"I was told I wasn't worth anything. I was told I was an ugly, good for nothing piece of crap," she remembered. "He even told me that God wasted His time when He created me."

The abuse had grown so bad that Elizabeth ended up in the hospital after some of his violent tantrums. Her home was a war zone and he was the Enemy.

When she was seven months pregnant with their fourth child, he picked her up and body slammed her against the hard floor, knocking the wind out of her. One day she came home from work and found him in a bad mood. He slapped her and then pushed her to the ground again. Elizabeth tried to scream and get away, but she couldn't do either. He was too strong and too angry. He jumped on top of her, pinning her arms under his knees, so she could no longer fight back.

"He began choking me to the point where I almost blacked out," she shared, "but then all at once, he screamed in pain and loosened his grip."

At that moment, their oldest daughter, Mercedes, had jumped on his back and bit him as hard as she could. He grabbed her and threw her off of him, and she began whimpering. That's when Elizabeth knew she had to find the courage to take her children and leave him forever.

That was in December 1994. Just when she thought life couldn't get any harder, it did.

On January 5, Elizabeth was trying to make a new start, but her ex was still in the picture because they shared four children. As she drove to his apartment—where her children were visiting—she froze. The apartment was completely engulfed in flames, surrounded by fire trucks and ambulances. Elizabeth jumped out of her car and made her way through the thick, black smoke toward the apartment when a police officer stopped her.

"Are you the mother of the children inside the apartment?" he asked.

Elizabeth nodded yes. The officer led her to an ambulance. There, she saw a tiny yellow bag. Her seven-month-old had passed away in the fire.

Elizabeth collapsed with grief.

A fireman carefully placed the tiny lifeless body in Elizabeth's arms. She held her and rocked her as snow fell in Amarillo that afternoon.

As she fought to process what was happening, Elizabeth learned that her other children were en route to the hospital and she needed to go there at once. Her ex-husband went separately and was little support for her. She was led to a hospital room where four-year-old Mercedes lay on the bed, lifeless. Mercedes had passed away just minutes before. Elizabeth dropped to her knees.

"Where are my other children?" she screamed, running into the corridor.

"Your son and daughter are in ICU," a nurse informed her. When Elizabeth saw her babies, she hardly recognized them. They were covered in tubes and bandages and hooked up to so many machines, it took Elizabeth's breath away.

After speaking with a doctor, Elizabeth knew the next forty-eight hours would be critical—especially for her son, who needed to make the journey from Amarillo to Louisiana, where a pediatric heart specialist was standing by. But the snow continued to fall, making a care flight impossible that night. The minutes turned to hours, and before the weather cleared enough for takeoff, her son suffered a heart attack and died.

With three children already gone, Elizabeth sat with her three-year-old daughter. "You're a fighter, Marcella. Keep fighting, baby girl!"

Trying to prepare her for the inevitable, the doctor said, "It will be nothing short of a miracle of God for your daughter to make it."

But Elizabeth wasn't ready to give up on her daughter, or her God.

At the end of the week, Elizabeth's baby girl was still hanging on, so she instructed her family to plan the funerals for her other three children while she stayed at the hospital.

In the middle of all the loss and pain, more than five hundred people showed up at the funeral to support the family—hundreds of people they had never even met before.

"As we rode to the cemetery to say our final good-byes, people lined the sides of the road with their hands over their hearts," Elizabeth remembered. "Men took off their hats out of respect. The city of Amarillo seemed to grieve with us."

God had been silent throughout this horrific time in her life; she couldn't believe He would allow this to happen. But as days turned into months, and her daughter remained in a coma, she knew she needed divine intervention. The doctors had told her that even if Marcella survived, she would be a vegetable.

"She will never be the same again," one of the physicians said. "Do you understand?"

Elizabeth nodded yes, but that didn't mean she was ready to take her daughter off the machines that were sustaining her life. Cuddled up in a little chair next to her daughter's bed, Elizabeth stared out the window, focusing on a very bright star that hadn't been visible in previous nights. In that moment, she prayed, "God, if you are real, please help me."

Minutes later, all the machines attached to her daughter started beeping. Marcella was flatlining.

The tube that had been down her daughter's throat now dangled beside her. As one of the nurses tried to put it back in, another tried to remove Elizabeth from the room.

"No, I'm staying!" Elizabeth yelled.

Suddenly, all of the beeping stopped. In the silence, a small, squeaky voice could be heard.

"I'm thirsty. I want some water."

For the first time in three months, Elizabeth heard her daughter's voice. Marcella was not only awake, but she was speaking!

"I had my miracle," Elizabeth shared.

The doctors kept warning Elizabeth that Marcella might lose her vision, and that she might never walk again, but Elizabeth knew that God would finish the work He had begun in her daughter, and He did.

Elizabeth's ex-husband deepened his own turmoil by breaking, entering, and stealing while the kids were in the hospital. He attended the funeral of their children in a stolen car and was recognized. He was jailed for more than two years. During this time, Elizabeth fled to Dallas.

Marcella fully recovered; today she is a mom herself!

Elizabeth has finally come to terms with the loss of Robert, Angelica, and Mercedes, knowing she will see them again in heaven. And on those days when it's still tough, she thinks back on what God told her five years ago: "He said, 'Remember that night in Marcella's room? You asked me if I was real, to please help you. I answered your question by giving you a walking miracle to remind you every day that I am who I say I am. I have been with you the whole time—then and now.' That day, I asked God to heal me and use me for His purpose."

And He has.

Discovering strength in loss, Elizabeth has risen up to make a difference, founding STAND—Stand Together Against Nationwide Domestic violence. Using her testimony, she is reaching out to the brokenhearted, the hopeless, and those who have given up on God. She can truly say to them, "I've been where you are, and I'm here to tell you that God will make a way! He will use what the devil meant to kill you and turn it around for His glory. What He did for me, He will do for you."

In 2013, STAND hosted its first event in Arlington, Texas—a charity run honoring Officer Jillian Smith, who responded to a domestic violence call and was killed while helping the victim.

"Our mission is to bring domestic violence awareness to the community," Elizabeth said. "I do this so others don't have to go through what I went through, to help them and show them that there is a different life. . . . And it keeps my babies' memories alive."

She is standing on her life verse, Ephesians 6:10, which says: "Finally, be strong in the Lord and in his mighty power." "God is using me as a tool to help others," she shared. "And still I stand."

After reading Amy's and Elizabeth's stories of discovering strength in loss, we should all be encouraged, knowing if they can make it through such horrific circumstances and come out on the other side stronger, then so can we. What He did for them, He will also do for us.

You may not have lost a child like Amy and Elizabeth, but maybe you've suffered another kind of loss. Maybe you've lost your job, are grieving over the end of your marriage, are mourning the loss of a loved one, or you're simply sad over the death of a dream. Whatever your loss, it's real and it's painful. Take time to acknowledge the pain of your loss. Don't bury it like I did for so many years, because that's not healthy. When we do that, we often try to fill that void with things or people in an attempt to stop the pain, but only God can fill it.

No matter what kind of loss you're dealing with today, nothing is too big for God. He can repair hearts. He can resurrect dreams. He can restore marriages. He can do whatever needs to be done, and here's the really good news: He wants to! All you have to do is ask and believe.

The Bible says we have not because we ask not (James 4:2), so ask Him.

I know it's hard to trust Him when you feel like He has let you down by allowing the loss in the first place, but this is not the time to run away from God. It's the time to press into Him. He didn't cause the loss, but He will bring you out of your despair if you'll just call on Him like Elizabeth did. She simply prayed, "God, if you're real, I need help," and He showed up in a big way. Despite what some skeptics say, God is still a miracle-working God.

It's time to stop asking why, and it's time to start trusting God.

Pray this with me:

Heavenly Father, we come to you today in our brokenness, and we ask you to repair, restore, and resurrect those losses in our lives so that we can move forward—empowered and purposeful for you. In the Mighty Name of your Son, Jesus. Amen.

Power Points

- Your misery can become your ministry.
- God is on duty 24/7, and you have direct access to Him.
- We have not because we ask not—so ask!
- It's time to stop asking *why*, and it's time to start trusting God.

Power Prompters

- What is your greatest loss?
- Do you see a ministry being birthed from that misery? If so, what is it?
- Have you truly given God your hurts and disappointments surrounding the losses you've experienced in your life? If not, what is stopping you?

NINE
Stepping Out in Faith

Have you experienced a moment in church when you thought your pastor was reading your mind? Or had been listening in on your phone conversation with your sister or girlfriend? Have you had the feeling that, as God's truth is spoken to the audience, the message is specifically meant for you? It happened to me on one very special Sunday in February 2008.

As I talked about earlier in this book, watching Emmitt win the mirror ball trophy on *Dancing with the Stars* was filled with so many happy, proud, and joyful moments. But that mirror ball also reflected something about me: What was *I* going to do to be a champion? What would I do to stretch my skills and deliver something wonderful to the world? I had so much ambition but so little direction. I needed a word from God.

That Sunday in February, as I listened to Bishop Jakes deliver his sermon, I received a word. Bishop Jakes told the congregation, "I don't know what God has told you to do, but whatever it is, you better do it."

Bells went off. It felt like I was sitting in a spotlight. There were 7,500 people in church that day, but I knew God was talking to me.

113

"I don't know what God has told you to do, but whatever it is, you better do it."

I got chills. My eyes opened. I heard what God had been trying to tell me for years. In that defining moment, I was ready to listen. I was ready to receive God's message. More important, I was ready to move forward with my assignment.

My dear friend Donna and my spiritual mentor and sister Cathy were also at church. As soon as Bishop Jakes said those words, they came to me from their seats. Each woman, on her own, got the message that morning.

"Pat, did you hear that?" Donna asked.

"You *have* to do it," Cathy said. "The time is now."

They were right. With God's word, I just knew it was time to launch Treasure You.

This was one of the biggest, most important moments of my life—and to have witnesses in that special moment was so surreal. We think miracles of God were only in biblical times, but we have modern-day miracles all around us. This was one of my miracles.

The next day I called Millicent, my friend and event planner who has been a supporter of my idea for Treasure You from the very beginning. It was hard to believe that after that moment on the golf course in Pebble Beach (when I first had the idea of hosting a women's retreat), my dream was finally taking shape. Millicent and I had talked about Treasure You many times over the last couple years, and she was always my advocate, ready to plan and move on exciting ideas.

Now those ideas were going to be reality.

You may be wondering why it took me so long to get started. I can give you an answer with two words: the Enemy. He taunted me, telling me that I'd never be able to succeed, I wasn't good enough, and no one would come. That Enemy got to me in the past, and I let him persuade me.

But no more. Now God was leading the way.

Millicent and I set a date for the retreat and began looking for the perfect location. I knew that if I set the date, I couldn't turn back. My goal was to have the first event within three months. I put together a binder with ideas and inspirations. I knew exactly what I wanted the event to look like, feel like, and be like. I wanted to create an intimate, safe, loving, warm environment for women to open up, share, be themselves, and feel inspired. I narrowed down the locations to a few resorts in Arizona, and Millicent and I traveled to the first one. On paper, it seemed ideal. But once we arrived, I didn't have that "this is it" feeling. So we went to the next resort. We walked into the Royal Palms Resort and Spa in Phoenix, and it was heaven on earth. There were beautiful gardens overflowing with flowers. Private villas. Any spa treatment you could imagine. It felt like a sanctuary. Millicent and I looked at each other. We knew we'd found our place.

We stayed the night and went right into the event-planning details. We went over my wish lists of guests, all of whom were women married to high-profile men in business, sports, entertainment, politics, and religion. Our goal was to inspire these wonderful women, who were often in the shadow of their husbands, to live the life that God had purposed for them. My mission was to pamper and love on them so they felt treasured and safe to share.

We commissioned custom-made boxes that would serve as the envelope to the invitation. The boxes were gorgeous, covered in gems and silk fabric. I wanted "treasure" to be the theme, because I wanted these women to know they were treasured by God. My invitation read: *You are a treasure. It would be my honor to treasure you.* When one of the women responded, "I'd love to attend the Treasure You event," the words *Treasure You* resonated in my spirit.

And that's how Treasure You was officially named! That woman was Holly Robinson Peete, and she will forever be special to me for inspiring the name.

As we planned our first Treasure You event, I was focused on being obedient to God to fulfill His purpose for me. I was boldly jumping off that cliff. I was all in. Sink or swim. Success or fail. Every day, with every item on our to-do list, God's voice resonated in my spirit.

Everything was rolling. I loaded the agenda with high-profile speakers and guests that I thought would be a draw. We had over-the-top gifts and meals prepared by award-winning chefs. I assumed my guests would only want to come if there was someone exciting and influential to meet, so I delivered. The lineup included great pastors and ministers who I thought would ensure attendance.

All around me, I had the most wonderful support system: Cathy, my mentor; Ellen Miller, a dear friend, author, and marketing genius; and Tara Jackson, my best friend, who was in ministry school at the time. But throughout all of the planning, craziness, and stress, I didn't realize one critical thing. I never invited any of my inner circle to speak at my retreat. As I rushed to get the big names and the incredible gifts, I overlooked the fact that I had some of the most gifted people on the planet working right beside me. This would be an important realization in the near future—I just didn't know it at the time.

It wasn't long before the RSVPs started to come in. Most of the women who accepted were the ones I thought would be too busy to attend or uninterested. I was so excited! As the event drew nearer, everything was in sync. I had a great guest list, perfect location, and stellar speakers. All of those smaller details you need to successfully run an event, from guest transportation to room gifts, were falling into place. I was on track to have the most incredible Treasure You event I could've ever imagined.

But it only takes one little push for the dominos to fall.

The Tuesday evening before the event, I was in my bedroom packing. The plan was for Emmitt and me to fly to Arizona together so he could attend a business meeting during the time of my event. But while he was in the shower, the phone rang. It was his mother, whom we lovingly call Mimi. When I answered, she shared the news that Emmitt's baby brother, Emil, had passed away.

The news was devastating. I tried to comfort Emmitt. We were both distraught. I was hurting for me, for Emmitt, for Emil, and for the entire family. "I can cancel the retreat," I said. "We need to focus on this."

"Baby, you're not cancelling the retreat," Emmitt replied. "This is an assignment God gave you. I will still fly with you to Arizona. You're going to do this retreat. When you get back home on Sunday, we'll fly to Florida and go be with our family."

So that's exactly what we did. The next morning, we got on that plane and landed in Phoenix. We drove to our hotel room, an air of sadness and grief all around. But I had an assignment, and with Emmitt's support, I was going to host a wonderful retreat.

Once we checked in, my phone rang. The news wasn't what I wanted to hear. One of the speakers had to cancel due to a death in the family. I was stunned. In the midst of my grief for our family's loss, here was another. I gave my deepest condolences.

As I scrambled to figure out what to do, the phone rang again. More undesired news: Another speaker had to cancel because a family member had a medical emergency. My heart was broken.

I hung up the phone, feeling shell-shocked. The whole thing I worked so hard to create was crumbling. The Enemy went to work on me. "You are a failure," he said. "You never heard from God in the first place. This is something *you* wanted to do. People are going to laugh at you."

The Great Gazoo was relentless.

What took me three months to build was falling apart in an hour.

Cathy went straight to ministering to me. "This retreat is going to happen," she said. "It's going to be wonderful."

Cathy sprang into action. She worked it out so that she and Ellen Miller would serve as moderators. Pastor Pamela Hines called to check on me and see if I needed anything. I asked if she could conduct a prayer session on Saturday morning and she said yes. And my BFF agreed to host the icebreaker and share her testimony.

In the span of thirty minutes, we were back on track.

It was one of the most stressful, nail-biting lessons I'd had in a long time. I learned that when God is at work, He is not in awe. He created all of us, and He gave us our gifts and our purpose. I had to learn that the big name wasn't important—the message was. Although the amazing women who couldn't attend my retreat would have delivered incredible and inspiring messages, I know now that God was trying to teach me a lesson: Don't use people to draw others to me . . . only *I* can draw people to me. In such a short time, God wiped the slate clean, taking all but one of my speakers away, and then built things right back up. There was just one piece still missing: I needed a speaker to close out the event.

Back in the hotel room, my husband was quiet. He was in mourning. I was so scared about having to speak in front of everyone, but I didn't want to bother him with my troubles that were so insignificant by comparison. I retreated to the sitting area and sobbed. There, the Enemy clawed his way back in, sending messages of defeat, while at the same time I felt God in my spirit telling me to trust Him and ask Him for help. There was a battle going on in that chair! So I called out: "Jesus, I need you. Please help me. I feel such pain and agony over everything coming at me."

Just then Cathy called. I shared with her my worries concerning the retreat and the fact that I no longer had a closing speaker. She said, "You're going to close out your own retreat." I said, "There's no way." I had no experience and I was terrified. It took me enough courage to put together the retreat, and the thought of ministering and closing it out terrified me. I fought her, saying I couldn't do it, that it would be better if we had someone else, but she insisted I could. She told me to study Luke 8:43–48, which is known as the Woman with the Issue of Blood. The Scripture says,

> And a woman was there who had been subject to bleeding for twelve years, but no one could heal her. She came up behind him and touched the edge of his cloak, and immediately her bleeding stopped. "Who touched me?" Jesus asked. When they all denied it, Peter said, "Master, the people are crowding and pressing against you." But Jesus said, "Someone touched me; I know that power has gone out from me." Then the woman, seeing that she could not go unnoticed, came trembling and fell at his feet. In the presence of all the people, she told why she had touched him and how she had been instantly healed. Then he said to her, "Daughter, your faith has healed you. Go in peace."

The woman, who was very ill, had such a strong, unrelenting faith in Jesus that she knew if she could just reach out and touch His hem, she would be healed. So she pursued this knowledge, even though it was against the accepted norm. As I read this passage, I knew I needed to touch Jesus spiritually—I just needed to reach out to Him and ask Him to help and heal me. I needed to have faith and believe that even though everything was falling apart, God had given me this assignment, and I needed to lean on Him for healing and hope instead of wallowing in my pain. Just as the woman in the Scripture put all her faith and hope in Jesus, I needed to put all my faith in Him. I saw myself as that woman.

So I reached out to the Lord, and He immediately started restoring me and healing me and building me back up. It was a miraculous moment. I went to bed studying the Scripture, and when I woke up, I felt like a new person.

All because I believed He could cover me and take care of my situation. And He did.

That morning, I was ready to get to work. Cathy flew in to conduct an all-day training session with the team. It was important for us to be as prepared as we could.

"I'll be right here with you," she told me. "You're not alone."

I can't express enough how much I love Cathy. I'm eternally grateful for her guidance and love. I was nervous and a little worried, but mostly excited. This was going to be great.

The next morning when I woke up, I was a giggly little girl at Christmas. I couldn't wait for my guests to arrive. I sat in anticipation in the guest arrival area—that's how excited I was. We had mocktails, and I personally greeted each of my guests because I wanted them to feel my excitement over their presence.

As the day began, I took a moment to reflect. I learned that it's one thing to have faith when everything is working to your advantage. But what are you going to do when things start going wrong?

I turned once again to Proverbs 3:5–6: "Trust in the Lord with all your heart and lean not on your own understanding; in all your ways submit to him, and he will make your paths straight."

I trusted in the Lord, submitted to Him, and obeyed. And I'm happy to report that the first Treasure You retreat was amazing. The weekend was filled with laughter, spiritual breakthroughs, healing, and restoration. God did a great work.

One of the volunteers told me afterward that her life was changed forever by witnessing the experience. She saw the things we had to overcome when it looked like we were in trouble, and she was inspired by what we achieved. And gospel singer and radio host Yolanda Adams, who wasn't present until Sunday, ministered through words and music so powerful and on target you would have thought she had been involved in every session. This is the work of God.

I want to share another piece of feedback from the attendees. Remember when I said I worked hard to get a lineup of well-known speakers and over-the-top events and gifts because I believed that was the only way these high-profile, busy women would ever want to come? I was wrong. Many told me they came to the event because of the potential for camaraderie, sisterhood, and restoration.

I was immediately humbled and grateful to God.

I left that weekend on a supernatural high. I flew to Florida and grieved with my family, helping Emmitt and everyone as much as I could. When I returned to Dallas, word had spread about the success of the event. This is when I realized that all women from all walks of life need to experience a Treasure You retreat. And this is when I opened my heart and mind to expanding Treasure You into what it is today. God gave me the second chance to create Treasure You, and then took it beyond my imagination.

When we open our hearts and minds and let God in—when we step out in faith—we can achieve great things. Sometimes it's scary to take on a new challenge, particularly when the Enemy fills our minds with doubt. But when we take that doubt and twist it into faith and determination, there's no limit to what we can accomplish. The story of my dear friend Michelle Lentz is proof. I've known Michelle for years, and I've watched her journey up close and personal.

It was only about three years ago when Michelle was, as she says, "Not in a good, healthy place" in her life. She was overweight, depressed, insecure, stressed out, and dealing with negative family members. On top of all of this, her father was battling breast cancer. (Yes, men get breast cancer—about one in a thousand are diagnosed with the disease.)

As Michelle went about her daily life, the discontented feelings continued. Her husband had lost 125 pounds, and she longed to look and feel as good as he did. She felt jealous of his ability to take care of himself. "I had mom guilt and felt that I couldn't leave my family to go do something for myself," she said, "even though my husband encouraged me to."

It wasn't until one afternoon when she saw photos of herself that she realized change had to happen. "I was going through pictures of an amazing Disney vacation we had taken the kids on, and I noticed that I was in only a few. In those pictures, I was bigger than my husband, and I looked so unhealthy and miserable."

It was a rude awakening of sorts, and Michelle was fed up. She knew she needed to lose weight, take better care of herself, and reprioritize her career. When one of her clients told her about a line of nutrition and weight-loss products, Michelle saw the opportunity to make a change, and quickly signed up for the program. With better food choices and supplements that helped her control cravings, the weight came off. Her goal wasn't to lose a specific number of pounds or reach a certain pants size. All she wanted was to feel better. At the end of three months, Michelle had lost forty-five pounds.

"I felt amazing and had more energy than I knew what to do with," she said. "So I began finding time to go to the gym, and even though it was a quick thirty minutes, it was a time for me to refocus, recharge, and reconnect with myself and deal with all the emotional baggage I was carrying around. What came from it was a whisper—a whisper that I had more to give."

As she lost weight and gained confidence, Michelle's desire to launch her own business grew. Fear reared its ugly head, as it often does, and held her back. That is, until she met a woman who inspired her.

"She said she was fearless," Michelle said. She even wore a bracelet with the inspirational word, almost like a daily reminder. At first, Michelle thought *fearless* meant her new friend wasn't afraid of anything and was willing to jump into something without thinking about the consequences.

But that wasn't what fearless meant at all.

"After making serious life changes and doing some soul searching, I came to the realization that what she meant by *fearless* was believing and trusting in a power bigger than ourselves. Fearless is leaving fear in God's hands. It sounds so simple, but at the time, the fear was eating me alive and I didn't know how to deal with it."

Michelle shared her fears with her good friend and life coach.

"Her advice was to listen to what was stirring inside me and not to be afraid. She said to be prepared and ready for whatever He has in store, and just walk up to the edge. He will push you if and when it's meant to be."

Six months after she began her weight-loss journey, Michelle felt the push. She left her job of fourteen years and started her own business. "Before I knew it, He had shoved me off that edge and I was falling into what is now my new career, my new life, with such freedom and calm I didn't have before."

Michelle's experience, from weight loss to finding the courage to start her own company, was life-changing. Today, she says she has a new purpose.

"My passion is to pay it forward and inspire other women to dream big, love life, and uplift one another. My purpose is to show what is possible when you are fearless—and how important it is to love yourself first."

So what fears are holding you back? When you relinquish those fears by stepping out in faith, you too can find new passion and purpose in your life. Paying attention to God's message changed my life, and He has led me to help thousands of women through Treasure You. It is God who inspired me to write these words to you now. I had to be ready to hear the message and feel it in my spirit. Once that happened, I was ready to jump forward. God led me to this point in my life, and I am doing His work. God taught me the importance of stepping out in faith; He will do the same for you.

How do you hear God's voice? I've never heard His audible voice. But I've heard Him speak through other people, through His Word, a stirring in my spirit, and sometimes even with chills. John 10:27 says, "My sheep listen to my voice; I know them, and they follow me."

It takes a while to trust it, and the Great Gazoo is going to make you question yourself whenever he can. Faith is like a muscle—you have to build it. God spoke to me the day I was on the golf course with my sister. And while I knew then that I wanted to make Treasure You a reality, my faith wasn't strong enough to receive God's message. But years later, when Bishop Jakes said it, I was ready. It was clear as all get-out.

When you are stepping out in faith, the Enemy may try to weasel his way in. Remember, he's on an all-out mission to stop God's great work. With me, he worked every angle to thwart God's plans. But he did not prevail.

I've learned on my journey that if you are obedient, no matter how difficult things get, and no matter what the Great Gazoo is saying in your ear, there will be many blessings that flow for you and others. When God gives you an assignment, He's already worked through the plan. All you have to do is listen, follow His directions, and go. Treasure You is proof. As a Christian woman, being able to see God's work is a blessing. To date, we've hosted thousands of women at Treasure You events, and we're just getting started. This is the power of God.

Lean on Him and be bold, even when it sounds out of range or too big for you. After all, we don't want the stuff we can accomplish on our own. We want the stuff we can accomplish only through God.

Power Points

- We tend to think miracles of God are only found in biblical stories, but keep your eyes open for modern-day miracles all around you. You are a miracle!
- Be obedient and open to what God is telling you. Listen to His voice and receive it in your spirit—and then move into action.
- We don't want the stuff we can accomplish on our own. We want the stuff we can accomplish only through God.

Power Prompters

- Is there a dream or goal you're afraid to pursue?
- Has there been a time when God spoke to you but you were too fearful to receive the message?
- Has there been a time when you heard God's voice and acted upon it?

TEN

Practicing Powerful Prayer

Several years ago, a woman named Joy Hill approached me after church and asked if I was interested in joining a new woman's prayer group focused on praying for husbands who frequently travel.

"God put your name on my heart to invite," she told me.

Joy was one of The Potter's House worship leaders, so I knew who she was, but I didn't know her on a personal level. I was cautious about the offer since it involved talking about my husband to people I didn't know. Still, the idea of belonging to a prayer group like this touched my spirit. So I called Tammy Franklin, one of our mutual friends, and asked her what she thought. She said that Joy was amazing and that I should join the prayer group. So, with Tammy's stamp of approval, I did. And after being a part of this group for many years, I can affirm that the experience has been life changing.

When we first came together as a group, Joy set boundaries and ground rules. We had to be on time. No food would be served at our meetings, just water and juice. The group would meet for one hour monthly, each time at a member's house. Joy made sure we were all 100 percent clear on the group's purpose: We were here to worship and pray, not vent about our husbands! Our studies began by reading a book by Pamela Hines called *A Wife's Prayer*. Each month, we'd read a chapter, discuss it as a group, and then end the session by praying out loud together.

Over the years, this prayer group has evolved from a sisterhood of women coming together to pray into a group of women who have a unique spiritual bond and connection. We celebrate birthdays, have our own Treasure You Moments and spa days, and we've even taken overnight trips together. We are true sisters and girlfriends. We have grown together spiritually. We have counseled each other through the many different seasons of our marriages. We have helped each other deal with family matters and deaths. And most important, we are heart-connected through prayer. I feel so blessed to say that not one woman has ever betrayed another prayer group sister.

Joining was one of the best decisions I ever made. Thanks, Joy!

Prayer is one of God's greatest gifts, and its power to heal and fulfill is amazing. And when you share prayers with others you trust, the power builds. It's so awesome to know that through praying with people, you can be that close. That's the work of God, and it's beautiful. It was during a powerful prayer group time that I had the revelation that I hadn't truly healed from my mother's death, and instead of looking for a way to fill the hole, I needed to allow God to heal me. This sudden understanding, which I felt deep in my spirit, changed my life.

When you participate in a prayer group, you are, in some ways, putting yourself in a vulnerable position. You're sharing your feelings, your beliefs, your convictions, your struggles, and your concerns. You're also opening yourself up, sometimes even exposing your deepest emotions. It was for this reason that my sister and girlfriend Melani Ismail first shied away from joining our prayer group.

"I thought about my privacy and not wanting to have that level of openness with anyone," she said. "There is a different vulnerability when you open up spiritually than when you put out spiritually. I only had that level of vulnerability with my mother."

But Joy was persistent in her attempts to help Melani realize what she could experience, and eventually Melani joined our group. Over the years, she's sought advice, found comfort, or relied on sisterhood for issues related to her marriage troubles, the death of her father, and raising her children. She says she has learned something from every person in our prayer group.

Here is another reason why prayer groups are so special: They are the foundation for true, unyielding friendships. "This group matured me as a woman," Melani said. "I have become more accountable in my friendships. I have learned how important it is to carry and hold a secret. I learned that you have to be a secret keeper. And I learned to RSVP!"

It's the bonding that changed Melani, she said. "Your friendships should teach you to be better, not tear you down. . . . It's a great place to learn how to be a friend."

As our group grew closer year after year, we made the decision to refrain from expanding our circle. We wanted to preserve the special dynamic we have. (But because we knew firsthand how powerful prayer groups are, all of us agreed to help anyone who wanted to form her own group.) It's amazing that the most simple thing—prayer—can bring people together on such a deep level. Prayer unites us and connects us to one another—and the Lord—in the most special ways. "For where two or three gather in my name, there am I with them" (Matthew 18:20).

A marriage can be its own prayer group, and this act of being together in front of God strengthens the union. There have been several times throughout my sixteen-year marriage when my sister has asked me, "Are you and Emmitt praying together?"

When you've been married for as long as Emmitt and I have, you're going to have struggles that are born out of miscommunication or frustration, but coming together to pray will break down those issues holding you back as a couple so you can go before God.

I'll admit there are times when I'm hurt or angry and want to pray with my husband, and then Gazoo starts talking in my ear, discouraging me. But I have learned, as I mentioned in a previous chapter, that it is important to "push through the pain" and make that extra effort to pray together.

Praying together doesn't have to be some elaborate ceremonious gesture. It just needs to be genuine and pure. Emmitt and I sometimes pray together first thing in the morning. We lie in bed on our backs and hold hands, or we kneel side by side. We start our prayers with whatever comes to mind, and we take turns going first. If we're in a hurry—like he's rushing out to a big meeting or if I've got something important that day—we'll face each other, hold hands, and quickly pray together. Prayer has become a huge part of our marriage and our union.

When I pray, even if it's just a quick, "Help me, Lord," I feel God swoop in and relieve me of a burden or fear or anxiety. With prayer, I feel a calmness and a peace in my spirit.

One of the most important pieces of advice I can offer for praying couples is to be aware of how you actually say your prayers. Avoid becoming an accuser in the prayer. Don't say things like, "I pray that my husband would stop being so self-ish," or "I pray that my husband would tell me I'm beautiful more often." Pray for your betterment as a wife and his as a husband. Ask God to help you communicate better, listen to each other more, and grow together. Be specific. God already knows what you need, but He wants you to have the faith to believe that if you and your spouse come together before God, He will hear you.

Practicing powerful prayer is a family affair, too. Any time my children go through a difficult time, I make sure we pray together. For example, after the first day of her freshman year of high school, Jasmin came home from school, collapsed, and cried. I asked her what was wrong, but she couldn't put her feelings into words. I said, "Look, baby, let's pray." And we went into heavy, deep prayer. I've done that with her and all of my kids in critical moments so that they start to learn the power of prayer. I want them to learn that I love them and their daddy loves them, but that God loves them more.

Growing up, I went to my mother for everything. I didn't have a relationship with the Lord. As a mother, I want to do everything I can to be sure that my children understand they have the same access to God as I do. I want them to know that if something happens to me, God will still be there for them.

The greatest gift I can give my children is their own relationship with God.

———————

Another way I've witnessed the power of prayer is through a community. This past year, my daddy suffered from a number of health problems related to his heart and lungs. He had emergency surgery, spent time in the intensive care unit, and at one point, relied on a ventilator. During this difficult time, I relied on prayer for strength. I reached out to anyone I could through social media and asked for prayers for my daddy. The responses were so powerful. I'd never gone to social media for support in that way, but the outpouring of love lifted my spirit. I'd sit in the hospital waiting room and read the comments and the promises of prayer from friends and people I didn't even know. I reached out to the congregation at my church and his church in Virginia. I asked anyone and everyone to pray for my father. And it wasn't long before I saw my daddy come back whole to the place he was before he fell ill. . . . And it was unbelievable.

Today, my father is back to playing bingo and participating in church activities, all with his girlfriend, Irma, whom I call Sweet Angel, by his side. Most important, he's living his life again. I got to see the miraculous power of prayer through him. There were so many issues with his health, but one by one they were uncovered and fixed. That an eighty-eight-year-old man could come back from all that he went through is pretty amazing. It's the power of prayer at work.

As for my own private prayer time, I make sure to have quiet time every day. My prayer time is in the morning. I go into my closet, get on my knees, and I talk to God, or sometimes I just let Him talk to me.

Psalm 46:10 says, "Be still, and know that I am God; I will be exalted among the nations, I will be exalted in the earth."

Every day I ask God to cover me, and I ask Him to help me keep Him first in every thought and decision. I ask Him to cover my family and protect them and shield them. I ask for forgiveness for my sins and for help with issues I'm struggling with.

When you take time to pray to God, remember that it doesn't have to be a long, elaborate, formal conversation. He knows us already, so if we go before Him and become someone else, He's not going to be fooled. When I talk to God, I talk to Him as Pat, and I believe that's exactly what He wants from us. Talk to God with reverence, but just be yourself.

Practicing powerful prayer doesn't just happen when you need something from God. Remember to pray to show Him thankfulness and gratitude. Thank Him for the food on your table, your spouse, and your family. Give Him thanks for all things. Your conversation with God doesn't have to be just about something that's wrong. After all, there are a lot of great things happening in our lives every single day. He already knows this, but He loves to hear the praises from our lips.

Power Points

- Praying with people you trust increases the power of prayer and forges strong relationships, especially with God.
- The greatest gift we can give our children is their own relationship with God.
- Ask God for strength and guidance, but also remember to thank Him and give praise for all of the good and challenging things in your life.
- Talk to God with reverence, but be yourself. He already knows you. . . . He created you.

Power Prompters

- If you don't practice powerful prayer every day, make a commitment to talk to God, whether it's to ask for help or to praise Him for your blessings.
- Ask your spouse if you can pray together.
- What prayers has God already answered in your life?
- What blessings can you thank God for in your prayers?

ELEVEN
Choosing to Never Give Up

For as long as I can remember, I dreamed of hosting a national morning news program or talk show. In my hometown of Chesapeake, Virginia, the local news anchors were our celebrities. I was captivated by them, longing for the day when I too would sit with interesting guests, talking about intriguing topics related to lifestyle and politics. When I went to college, I majored in journalism, training myself to follow in the footsteps of Katie Couric, who's also from Virginia. I watched her on *Today*, impressed by how real she was.

And then there was Oprah. I wanted to *be* Ms. Winfrey. In college I dressed like her—scarves, poufy hair, etc.—and watched her show as often as I could. I studied her interview style, the way she introduced her guests, and, of course, the way she dressed. She was real, just like Katie. Oprah took hosting to a new level. Her shows inspired and educated. There were days when my mommy would run home from work early just to catch the show.

"Baby, you can do a show like that!" she'd say. "We just need to get you an internship with *Oprah*."

"How am I going to do that?" I replied, knowing that Oprah—and her show—were entirely out of my reach. "Who do we know?"

She'd say she knew a Dr. So-and-So who met Oprah one time . . . and maybe he could pull some strings. (If only Dr. So-and-So could! That's just how mommies are—strong in their belief that their babies can do anything in the world!)

As an ambitious young woman, I was drawn to broadcasters like Katie and Oprah. They were my idols. And the desire to host a TV show that started in my hometown stayed with me for my entire life. So when I had the opportunity to co-host a local morning show called *D: The Broadcast* in February 2013, I was so thrilled. It was a dream fulfilled.

And it only took forty-two years to get there.

When I moved to L.A. in my twenties, I brought along all of my big dreams about a career in television. Then, I had no idea how many close calls I'd experience. Today I can't even count how many opportunities were just beyond my grasp. One of the biggest near-hits happened in 1998. I filmed a pilot for a national syndicated talk show called *Pat and Kat*, my co-host being then-up-and-coming comedienne Katsy Chappell. We had trained with an Olympian mind-set for the show, spending weeks on end perfecting our hosting techniques, producing segments, booking guests, and putting together wardrobes. But that year, another funny lady—this one much more well-known than Kat or me—was also in negotiations for her own show. As a result, *Pat and Kat* never aired. The distribution company went with *The Roseanne Show*. Losing out on that opportunity was difficult. I was *this close* to being where I wanted to be. But just as I'd experienced years ago as first runner-up in the Miss USA Pageant, only one can take the crown.

Close, but not quite there. Again.

Still, I persevered, going on audition after audition, taking acting classes, and attending workshops. In L.A. there are way more no's than yes's, but there were enough small victories to keep me hopeful: a guest appearance on *The Wayans Brother*s, a one-line appearance on *Beverly Hills, 90210*. I even filmed a commercial for Pizza Hut that was set to air during the Super Bowl. I played an anchorwoman. Talk about irony! However, the producer filmed two versions of the commercial, and guess whose version got cut? The world would never see my enthusiasm for Pizza Hut pizza!

Close, but not quite there. Again!

So there I was, positive and hopeful, diligent and dependable . . . and I was just squeaking by. I was doing my thing—but not really doing it well. I didn't know how long I could keep being disappointed.

As I explained earlier, I was living in L.A. when I started dating Emmitt. Around the time we were getting serious in our relationship, a potentially serious role came my way. I was being considered for a part on the daytime drama *All My Children*. I remember being so worried about what to do. If I got the part, I'd have to live in New York City, but Emmitt was in Dallas. How could I choose? I turned to God for guidance, telling Him to help me see which way to go. He did. The role ultimately went to another woman. Ironically, she was from Dallas.

With all of the trials and failures, I started to reevaluate my career goals. I reasoned that things weren't meant to be. If I was destined for a career in TV, wouldn't it have happened by now? I didn't see then that I was making decisions based on incomplete information. I thought I should have my career according to my timeline. As we all know, that is never the case. We all work on God's timeline.

Once I moved to Dallas and no opportunities came my way, I just let my dream go. I figured if I didn't want it anymore, then I couldn't be disappointed anymore. I wouldn't feel the sting from another "no."

Years later, I had a pivotal life moment while I was traveling to Los Angeles to watch Emmitt on the *Dancing with the Stars* All-Star Season. As I sat on the plane, I watched a DVD of Pastor Sheryl Brady preaching at the Woman Thou Art Loosed conference. (The event had taken place in Atlanta, and I had wanted to attend but couldn't because I was on tour with Women of Faith.) Her sermon focused on not giving up on your dreams. And as I sat in my seat, I realized that what Sheryl was saying applied to me. While I'd been so focused on making Treasure You a success, I still had this pull on my spirit to work in television. I just ignored it. Been there, done that. But as I watched the video, I had an eye-opening moment when I realized that when Sheryl was talking about people giving up, she was referring to me. I. Gave. Up. I did it to avoid feeling disappointed and hurt when things didn't go the way I wanted. Again, I wanted things to happen on my timeline. But as I sat on the plane, I knew with all of my heart that I didn't want to give up on TV. The desire and dream were still there.

I listened to Sheryl, and I felt like God was speaking to me. I'd given up on my dream for all the wrong reasons. As the plane landed in L.A., I was filled with excitement and a new energy. The moment I could use my phone, I called my first agent. I asked if we could meet.

I was in her office the next day. I told her I wanted back in.

"I don't know what's out there anymore," I said. "But I'm open to whatever could be a fit. Please just keep me in mind."

She said she would.

I headed back to Dallas. When I got home, Emmitt's agent called me. She told me there was an opportunity in Dallas for a new morning show hosted by four women. It was going to be like *The View*, but local. There was no name for the show yet, and she didn't know many of the details, but they wanted to meet with me.

"Are you interested?" asked the agent.

I couldn't say yes fast enough.

Well, as God would have it, the next day I got a second call about the same show. Bri Crum, a public relations executive I knew, said *D Magazine* was co-producing the show and wanted to meet with me in person to see if I'd be interested in hosting. This opportunity was coming at me from all directions! I met with Brian Joyce from the station and had a screen test with the other women being considered as hosts: Courtney Kerr, known for her fashion blogs and TV show on Bravo; Lisa Pineiro, a former news anchor; and Suzie Humphreys, former radio and TV personality and current inspirational speaker and humorist.

The four of us had instant chemistry. Before I knew it, I had an offer!

Once the deal was signed, we got to work: introductory videos, photo shoots, publicity interviews. The pace was fast, and I was excited. The night before the show first aired, I was crazy nervous. I didn't sleep at all. The dream I had since I was a little girl was coming true all these years later—in my forties with five kids and living the married life in Dallas. I never thought it would come along now! I was so appreciative that God would give me the opportunity to do a live morning show. And the logistics were so perfect. The studio was just five minutes from my house! God gave me the opportunity to get up in the morning, see my kids off to school, and be at the studio at 8:30 a.m. I was finished by 10 a.m., with plenty of time to take care of my family and Treasure You responsibilities. God is great!

The inaugural show of *D: The Broadcast* aired on February 18, 2013. I was honored to be a part of it for seven months.

The training and experience I received were invaluable. Never before had I been given the opportunity to do live TV every day with teleprompters and guests and other hosts. Through this experience, I had the chance to confirm that I loved hosting television. I got to spread my wings and practice in a safe, fun, interesting environment.

I learned and grew in an area I always dreamed of working in. It was a boot camp experience that taught me so many things. Before God takes you to where He wants you to go, He will guide you through the steps and stages of preparation. For me, this was a preparation assignment, not my destiny moment.

When I think about all of the wonderful women I've met through Treasure You, one name stands out as someone who refused to give up on her dreams, even in the face of unbelievable obstacles. This precious woman embodies the drive, tenacity, and never-ending belief that God will lead us to the right path. Today, LaToya Brown shows us how far we can all go when we choose to never give up.

LaToya's childhood was filled with betrayal and sadness. When she was just nine years old, she was molested by her mother's boyfriend, leaving her with self-hate and thoughts of suicide. Two years later, her mother moved in with another boyfriend, leaving LaToya and her siblings behind. They stayed with a relative, then another, and then whoever else welcomed them. At one point, LaToya had to live with one of her mother's friends, who was addicted to crack cocaine. With no real role models or adult guidance, she was largely on her own when it came to food, clothing, and hygiene.

At age thirteen, LaToya had her first child. She moved into an apartment with her sister, and worked to balance motherhood with school. The next year, she was pregnant again, and during her pregnancy, she was sexually assaulted by someone in the neighborhood. Years of physical abuse taught her to cope in her own way. "I felt that the only way for me to control what happened to my body was to put something in my mind that no one could ever take away—my education."

The next few years brought more moves and more temporary stays with family and friends. She even lived for a while with her son's father, enduring mental and physical abuse to provide for her kids.

"In spite of my trials, I knew that I wanted to have a better life for me and my sons and was willing to sacrifice everything to make that happen."

As a high school senior, LaToya was pregnant with her third child. Her life was still filled with verbal abuse, this time from teachers, classmates, and neighbors. "The only motivation I had to help me overcome the obstacles I faced was my three sons," she explained. "I refused to be what others said about me, and I determined to be more than I thought could be. My faith in God and my faith in the future encouraged me daily to never give up."

Through a support group called Teens as Parents & Students, LaToya met a counselor. "She was the first person in seventeen years to ask if I had ever been abused," LaToya said.

LaToya graduated from high school, and with her counselor's encouragement and support, she enrolled in Mountain View Community College. The counselor and her husband bought LaToya a car, and Kathy's church helped the young mother furnish her first apartment. LaToya graduated from the University of Texas at Arlington in 2004 with a master's degree. She plans on getting a doctorate degree next.

"Many declared me a failure. Many said that I would be a statistic and would be on welfare my entire life. Many stated that my sons would be dropouts and inmates before they were teens," she said. "I'm so glad that I didn't listen to the 'many.'"

Whether your dream takes one year, one decade, or one lifetime, never give up. God has a plan for you. He will provide, and it will come to pass. Choosing to never give up, as LaToya did, will lead you to the greatness God has planned. I'm reminded again of Jeremiah 29:11, and encourage you to commit it to memory: "'For I know the plans I have for you,' declares the Lord, 'plans to prosper you and not to harm you, plans to give you hope and a future.'"

Power Points

- We all work on God's timeline, not ours.
- If you feel a pull in your spirit, follow it!
- Never give up on your dreams.

Power Prompters

- Have you given up on a dream because it hasn't materialized in the time and manner in which you thought it should?
- In what ways has God led you to realizing your dreams?
- What dream do you carry deep in your heart? And what are you going to do about it now?

TWELVE
Enriching Communication

Through sharing and positive communication, we often receive a second chance to enjoy the people who matter the most.

Ecclesiastes 4:9–10 says, "Two are better than one, because they have a good return for their labor: If either of them falls down, one can help the other up. But pity anyone who falls and has no one to help them up."

We all know the importance of communication. It's through this dialogue that we strengthen our relationships with each other and, most important, with the Lord. I often wonder why so many of us struggle to communicate with the people we love the most. Without communication, even the best relationship with a spouse, partner, friend, sibling, parent, or co-worker can be ruined. For this chapter, I'm going to speak mostly about my marriage, since this is one of the relationships (trust me, there are others) where I am challenged in terms of communication, but these insights can be applied to any significant relationship.

One of the most challenging decisions to make is choosing the right channel. I don't typically believe in using email or text messages to share my thoughts and feelings with friends and family. But on a rare occasion it has been a way to remove the emotion from a situation and help you both focus on the basics. But I would never do that with my husband. I generally believe if you have something important to talk about, do so in person or via phone. If you put this rule into practice, you'll reduce the possibility for miscommunication and misunderstandings. You'll also have a better chance of resolving issues more quickly and with less stress.

Emmitt and I have worked long and hard on enriching communication in our marriage, and although we have made great improvements, communication is a skill that requires continual focus and dedication. Last year, we experienced a communication breakthrough. Right around Father's Day, Emmitt opened up to me about his fears and anxiety for the future. He has always been a man driven to succeed, and he works so hard to provide for our family. But at that particular moment in time, he was worried about the future and his legacy. Instead of shutting down and withdrawing, as so many of us do when we are distressed, he chose to open up.

Now, I never thought of Emmitt as someone who had fears, so if he hadn't chosen to share, I wouldn't have understood why he was so quiet or withdrawn at times. When we talked, I not only learned about how Emmitt felt in that situation, but I understood my husband on a deeper level. And once I understood what he was worried about, I could support him and make sure I did things that met his needs, such as staying on budget. Talking about his concerns allowed me to have a greater sensitivity for his feelings. Experiencing that level of communication was special.

I want to make sure that I honor my husband's needs. Isn't that what you'd want for any relationship that's important to you? I'd like to share some of the things I've learned from my mistakes in hopes that it will help you with your everyday communication.

Counseling Is for Good Times and Bad

It's good to ask someone who's been through an experience how they did it. As a mother, I've gone to other people who have a similar challenge or situation with their child. I ask friends for advice, and in turn, they ask me. I encourage you to talk to people who have traveled down the same road as you so they can help you manage your expectations, deal with challenges, or avoid pitfalls.

Some of the best marriage advice I've ever received came from a couple whose marriage ended in divorce. When the wife (my friend) told me the news, I was surprised. From the outside, I thought they had an amazing marriage. They encouraged us to learn from their broken union by staying in counseling through good times and bad. They told us to think of our marriage as a car that needs maintenance checks, even when it's running fine. In a marriage, you're always working through something, even when nothing's wrong.

Heeding advice from this couple who divorced, Emmitt and I have been in counseling for years to make sure we are doing everything we can to stay connected. While I'm usually the one who's more forthcoming with my feelings and needs, I've noticed that Emmitt has become much more open over the years, and I know counseling has helped.

Establish Ground Rules

I've learned to establish communication ground rules. (Again, this doesn't pertain only to spouses, but rather it can be applied to relationships with siblings, friends, parents, and others.) One of the rules Emmitt and I have is that if we need to talk about something, we ask, "Please let me know when it's a good time for us to discuss some things." This simple request is a signal to the other person that there's a matter that needs to be resolved. Before we established this rule, we had the tendency to interrupt each other at inopportune moments to discuss issues. The solution to avoiding this misstep is to ask the other person for a good time to talk. This way, we have each other's full attention and come ready to listen. When you want to resolve something, you need to make sure you're in agreement about the timing so you can both benefit from the conversation.

Watch Your Tone

It's essential to pay attention to your tone and your emotions. Emmitt and I try to watch our tone with each other any time we talk. I can be overly emotional, and he can get fired up—or, as he calls it, "passionate"—but we've learned to talk when we're both calm.

When I was younger, I was much more feisty and impulsive than I am now. I thought every issue needed to be handled right away. Now I've learned to hold on to it and we deal with it later, when we both are in a good place and have the time and ability to focus. We have kids and people around us all day long, and we do a lot of business together. In the past, we've had moments of disagreement in front of others, but we realized that's not fair for anyone else, so we've learned to be aware of our tone with each other and handle issues offline.

Close friends and siblings are often guilty of getting overly emotional with each other, but communication will be much better received if it's delivered with a fair tone. I know that my sister and I have learned over the years to manage our tone in our discussions. This allows us to truly hear each other.

Timing Is Everything

On the journey to enrich communication, you have to remember that timing is everything. We wait for the kids to go to bed, and then we set up a meeting to talk, usually in our home office. We try not to have discussions or meetings in our bedroom. The bedroom should be a sanctuary.

No matter who you're communicating with, be sure to respect his or her time, and let the person know that you expect the same courtesy.

Write It Down

When you have your meeting, come prepared. Emmitt and I have learned to write things down that we want to discuss so we can stay on track, cover everything, and leave the conversation feeling like we've voiced the points we needed to. Not that you want to keep a tally of wrongs, but writing down things that need to be discussed helps you to remember your points.

Make Your Own Point

When a person calls a meeting, he or she gets to lead it. The other person can't take over or change the focus. Resolve the issue on the table before moving on to other topics.

Tell Your Spouse/Important Person What You Need

This may be the most important of all the communication lessons I've learned. Telling each other what we need has improved my marriage in big ways. For example, my husband loves coming home to a home-cooked meal, and he loves his wife's cooking. I know home cooking reminds him of his childhood.

His mother made a hot breakfast every morning—eggs, bacon, grits, biscuits—and when I cook it reminds him of the comfort of home and family. He doesn't ask for it every day, but I know it's important to him, so I do it as much as I can. However, as my life has gotten busier, I've communicated my needs . . . and one is to *not* feel the pressure to cook every day. Together, we reached a compromise where he's gracious and understanding, and I do my best to cook when I can.

For me, I love words of affirmation. I love when my husband tells me he loves me or that I'm a great wife or a great mother. I love for him to recognize what he sees as good in me or share how he feels about me.

What you need might be big things or simple gestures. It's important to remember it's a process and that you are always and forever working to enrich communication.

Sharing your needs isn't just for spouses; it's important for relationships with friends and family, as well. Since our friendship began in 1991, my BFF Tara and I have learned the importance of communicating our needs. We met as sorority sisters, and we've become closer with every year. But because we're completely opposite in a lot of ways, sometimes the way I think is different from Tara, or the way I come to a decision is much different from the way she would have reached a decision. We have learned to appreciate these differences, but only after putting a priority on talking things through.

One of the defining moments in our friendship came when I started dating Emmitt. For years, Tara had been my main confidante, the person I went to with my troubles and fears. She is such a great listener, and sometimes we'd talk all day long (back when we had less hectic lives!). Then, when I met Emmitt, my focus changed. My calls to Tara were less frequent, and we saw each other a lot less. This, understandably, affected Tara.

"I felt a sense of loneliness. I was used to talking with you on a regular basis. I felt a sense of abandonment—a sense of 'What about me?'" Tara said. "It wasn't so much jealousy, because I wanted you to be in a relationship. . . . I just wanted as much time as we had before."

When Tara was vulnerable and shared her needs with me, that moment opened the door to deep communication that was so important to our friendship. She was frustrated with me, and had she not told me, I wouldn't have been aware of her needs. Tara was basically saying, "I miss you." And that was fair. By her sharing her feelings, it made me more aware that my friend needed me just as much as I needed her.

Through this situation with Tara, I learned that you can have different opinions and views than your friends, and it doesn't diminish the closeness or importance of the relationship as long as you both commit to communication. You can't always do what your friend or family member wants or expects you to do, but when you truly care, you will want to make concessions and consider his or her point of view. Regular, open discussions are the key to enriching communication. And even though Tara lives in Maryland, we are committed to talking on a regular basis, and even make appointments when our schedules get busy. And when Tara met the love of her life, guess what happened? She was with *him* all the time! And this round, it was my turn to miss my friend. Today, Tara and I do what it takes to stay close. She's an integral part of my life, as I am in hers, so it's important for us to fight for that.

I've talked about my dear friend Millicent in previous chapters, explaining how instrumental she has been in supporting and facilitating Treasure You. One of the things I love best about Millicent is her willingness to listen to advice and try new things. Over the years, I've shared with her various situations and outcomes in my relationships, and we talk often about the role communication plays in our marriages and in our relationships with God.

So when Millicent and her husband, Gerald, went through a difficult season in their marriage and came out stronger and better than ever before, I saw just how important a role communication played in their relationship success.

Millicent and Gerald have been married for twenty-three years. They have a son in college and a daughter in high school. On the surface, they looked like the ideal family. But as Millicent will tell you, for several years, the reality was quite different.

In 2002, Millicent and Gerald were having financial troubles and marital struggles. Millicent was restless, feeling uninspired and bored with the relationship. So when she was offered a great job in Atlanta, the place where she and Gerald had previously lived, she rationalized that the opportunity was too good to pass up. She accepted the position, moving with her kids to the city. She told herself that Gerald could eventually move there, too.

Millicent became content with living apart from her husband. Then she grew fearless. She felt happy with her freedom and with the ability to support herself financially, and she didn't want to move back. Besides, she told herself, if push came to shove, she could always ask Gerald for child support.

But it wasn't long before Millicent came to realize that she needed to share her feelings with her husband. "I told him that I was bored and unhappy and explained what I needed," she said.

Armed with the knowledge that his wife was unhappy, Gerald did something wonderful: He fought for Millicent, insisting that they could make it work. Gerald suggested counseling, and he took the initiative to begin with his therapy first. After a while, Millicent and the children moved back to Dallas, and then she and Gerald attended counseling together.

"After five sessions, I walked out vowing to make it work," Millicent said. "My mother told me not to give up a lifetime for temporary emotions."

Counseling provided a safe, open environment for Millicent and Gerald to talk to a mediator who could share objective observations and provide input. This was a critical step in saving their marriage, and illustrates the importance of communication. However, even with the counseling road map, the couple still had to make a choice and a commitment to work on their relationship.

And they did just that. In the years since they attended counseling, Millicent and Gerald have been going strong.

"It's a rewarding sense of accomplishment," she said. "I'm thankful and I can't imagine having made a different choice. It gave me the attitude to never give up, and I'm looking forward to the next twenty years."

Millicent said that counseling taught her to speak up and share her needs. "It is important to make time to talk," she said. "I believed he changed, and I changed, by meeting each other's needs."

Making changes such as watching spending habits (Millicent) and putting more emphasis on talking and listening (Gerald) were two things the couple worked on.

"It's the little stuff that makes the big stuff matter," she says.

———————

How much emphasis do you put on enriching communication in your important relationships? Do you realize the power of words and the importance they have in the life you share with your spouse?

Ephesians 4:29 says, "Do not let any unwholesome talk come out of your mouths, but only what is helpful for building others up according to their needs, that it may benefit those who listen." As we discussed in chapter 10, prayer is a powerful way to speak to God and share your gratitude and struggles. This form of communication is the cornerstone to building your relationship with the Lord. To build relationships with others, you must also communicate. This is how your spouse, friends, and family members know you, understand you, and grow with you. Enriching communication is a skill that must be practiced and prioritized. But when you give it the attention it needs, the rewards are priceless. By enriching our communication, my husband and I have a stronger, deeper, richer relationship today than ever before. And I expect our relationship to continue to grow and evolve with each day because of our commitment to talking and understanding each other. We're actually due for a good sit down right now, but I'm patiently waiting for the right time.

Without communication, it's hard to have a second-chance opportunity with someone. Open dialogue, the right tone, and professional help if needed will lay the foundation for success.

I thank God that Tara and I, Millicent and Gerald, and, above all, Emmitt and I have learned the value of working through communication issues, learned each other's needs, and are experiencing second chances in our friendships and our marriages.

Power Points

- Communication is a skill that requires continual focus and dedication.
- Be honest about your needs and desires.
- Through sharing and positive communication, we often receive a second chance to enjoy the people who matter the most.

Power Prompters

- Schedule a meeting with your spouse, parent, friend, or sibling to discuss any issues you may have. Or just set aside time to talk.

- Make a list of three of your needs. Ask your partner to do the same. Then pick a mutually beneficial time to share the results.

- Recall a time when you and your spouse or another important person in your life successfully communicated to share thoughts and feelings or work through a situation. How can you replicate that success?

THIRTEEN

Learning to Treasure Yourself
(Regaining Your Power)

When I created Treasure You, my goal was to provide a community for women so that they would feel loved and inspired and have a safe environment to share. As it grew, it was important for me to raise money to help women who were in emergency financial need. Over the years, it has provided a path to help grow women's relationships with God. As I shared in chapter 5, "Finding Your Purpose," I was uncertain if such an organization would flourish, but Treasure You has been more successful than I could have ever imagined.

Treasure You is founded on the idea that we are to treasure the things of God, not the things of the world, and that every person deserves to be treasured and is a treasure from God. One of the things I've learned along this journey is that we all need to take time to treasure *ourselves*. The organization I initially created has grown into so much more. It is really a ministry and a way of living life to the fullest and affording second chances to women just like me!

All of us know the importance of loving and treasuring ourselves, but there are many times throughout our lives that we fall short of this mission. Maybe we are busy with work and family. Maybe we feel down. Maybe we are consumed with self-doubt or insecurity. I certainly have been in each one of those scenarios. But no matter how crazy, out of control, or off track our lives may seem, remember that God has a perfect plan for us and our lives. God created us, so we should make a commitment to appreciate who we are.

Genesis 1:27 says, "So God created mankind in his own image, in the image of God he created them; male and female he created them."

In a previous chapter, I shared my struggle with Emmitt competing on *Dancing with the Stars* and how I felt envious that it wasn't me selected to be on that stage. I was working so hard to be supportive and hold back my negative emotions that I forgot one of the most important people in the process: *me*. Where was my love for myself? I was so filled with sadness because of my own stalled career and jealousy over Emmitt's booming career that I got lost in my own shuffle. Over the years, I realized that his success didn't take away from mine. There wasn't a cap on the number of people who could succeed. There was plenty of room for me to achieve my goals, too. I had simply forgotten how.

When you treasure yourself, you aren't living your life through other people. I believe that we are all purposed and predestined for something special and significant. Many times, we lose ourselves in our spouse, our children, and our friends, and even as we care for elderly parents. We lose focus and forget our own purpose and special qualities. My feelings of jealousy, inadequacy, and insecurity in regard to Emmitt being selected for *Dancing with the Stars* weren't his fault. He had a great opportunity and he grabbed it. That he was bold enough to be on that stage is inspiring. Emmitt had never danced professionally before. He'd never done a television show like that before. And there was my baby, bringing down the house week after week.

Once I realized that his success didn't detract from mine, I made the conscious decision to stop my negative thoughts. His success empowered me to step out in faith, try new things, and pursue old dreams I had suppressed. I no longer wanted to live through him or anyone else. I was wallowing in what I didn't have rather than focusing on what I could have. As I watched Emmitt and others succeed, I learned that I too should feel empowered to follow my dreams. One of my dreams was to launch Treasure You. It wasn't long after that realization that I found the strength, passion, and direction to do it!

Now I feel God pulling me into a ministry that reaches even more people. The platform to minister through this book, speaking, social media, the world of print, broadcast TV, and the Internet present new opportunities to give hope and inspiration to others. I am so grateful and willing to go wherever He takes me!

I've met many people who say they are stuck because they get rejected in their pursuits. Not just in the entertainment business—although I can certainly understand that because I was told "no" more times that I can count—but with job interviews or attempts to achieve new personal heights. For those of us who work hard and continue to try to push down doors to make things happen, I want to share something I heard Tyler Perry say as he appeared on the NAACP Image Awards stage a few years ago. He said that we can receive a thousand no's, but just one yes from God can change everything. I often think about what he said, and I get excited for my upcoming one yes.

Maybe you've always wanted to dance, go back to school, play the guitar, learn to cook, or start your own business . . .

so go for it. Why not? Emmitt and his success weren't holding me back. *I was holding me back.* I realized I had the right to go to my husband and say, "I have this passion to build an organization that treasures women," or "I want to go back to TV." Whatever it is I want to do, I now am empowered to ask for support. And you should feel that way, too.

When I started treasuring myself and got busy with what I was called to do, I wasn't as troubled about what others were doing. As I worked toward the first Treasure You retreat, I had my focus back, and my energy was being spent in the way that God had intended. I know with Treasure You I found the path to my purpose. As I explained in chapter 9, "Stepping Out in Faith," I heard God's message for me one morning as I sat in church. In that moment, I knew I was ready to work hard to create this organization. But what happens if you don't yet know what your purpose is? While I can't say when God will deliver the message, or when you'll be ready to receive His word, I can tell you that your purpose will be something you love to do. It'll be something that makes you happy. It will give you a sense of fulfillment and peace. But you are the only one who can discover it.

From my perspective, you can get closer to finding your purpose by looking at the things you love to do so much that you'd do them for free. If you could do anything and not worry about paying the bills, what would you do? When you wake up each morning, what brings you joy and excitement? Now that I'm in my forties, I make decisions based on what I'm called to do rather than trying to please others. I've realized that when you do things that you aren't called to do, you are pulling focus away from what God has assigned for you.

Remember, Jeremiah 29:11 says, "'For I know the plans I have for you,' declares the Lord, 'plans to prosper you and not to harm you, plans to give you hope and a future.'"

When we slow down, listen, and are in a place to receive what God has planned for us, we can find fulfillment and peace. We are on assignment from God. By believing we are worthy of being treasured, and by taking steps to actually treasure ourselves, we can find and walk down the path that God intended for us.

———————

We all know that time, stress, family responsibilities, and other obligations can keep us from treasuring ourselves. This is why it sometimes takes a life-changing event such as a health scare for us to realize just how important it is to slow down. The story of my sister-in-love, Marsha Hill, is an example of just how difficult life can be when you don't take those crucial Treasure You Moments. If ever there was a woman who demonstrated the transformation from self-doubt to self-love, it's Marsha. She'll tell you her journey wasn't possible without God, and when you understand the ordeal this brave woman endured, you'll feel inspired to regain your own power.

Growing up, Marsha had people in her life who didn't show that they valued her. She tells the story of an aunt who verbally abused her, made her feel inferior to her cousins, and hurled insults and put-downs with no regard for Marsha's feelings. In school, Marsha was teased for being tall and skinny and having big eyes. She was called names. She said she never felt attractive but kept her insecurities to herself. Instead, she replayed a line she heard one Sunday in church: "There will be more stars in my crown when I get to glory." That one sentence served as an affirmation for Marsha, and it has helped carry her to this day.

After high school, Marsha drank and partied. "I gave some of the best parts of me away to men who didn't deserve me," she said. She met a man, and after a year and a half of dating, they married. But the relationship was troubled. He was materialistic and had a jealous heart, particularly toward Marsha's relationship with her family. "He felt like he had to compete with them," she said, adding that he was even jealous of her relationship with their first daughter, Marchelle. Before the birth of their second child, they moved to Corpus Christi, Texas, but the fresh start didn't change anything.

"I was miserable. He worked and played basketball with his friends, and I didn't know anyone. When we were mad with each other, we walked around the house for days—sometimes longer—not talking to each other. We weren't going to church, either," she revealed. "I felt alone at home. It was getting close to time for me to give birth to our second daughter, so I went back to Pensacola, Florida, to stay until after giving birth." She began to suspect her husband was having an affair. "I was in the ninth month of my pregnancy and wanted to see the Cowboys play the 49ers. He and my mom brought up a charter bus of Cowboys fans from Corpus Christi to see the game. At the beginning of the game he sat with Marchelle and me. During halftime he left, saying he would be back. After halftime, Marchelle began asking for her dad. My first thought was to go where our charter bus seats were; there I found him sitting between two women. It didn't look or feel right. I had an uncomfortable feeling in my stomach, and it wasn't the baby."

After giving birth, Marsha learned that her husband was indeed having an affair. Upon returning to Corpus Christi early one morning unannounced, she caught him walking out of their townhouse with the woman. After a heated argument, she packed her things and moved to Florida. He later married his mistress, but Marsha never looked back.

After the divorce, Marsha worked to get her life back on track. A few years later, she met Victor Hill, and despite the warning signs of infidelity, she married him. They had two children, but the marriage struggled. Even after Victor convinced Marsha he had cut off ties with his ex-girlfriend and his daughter, she still felt insecure and paranoid, regularly driving to his place of employment at four o'clock in the morning to make sure she saw his car at work. She was stressed out, suffered from blood pressure issues, and felt miserable and irritable. She thought about leaving, but the verbal insults from Victor and the thought of raising four girls alone was overwhelming.

So Marsha put on a happy face and pressed on for a while, but eventually she asked Victor for a divorce. "I felt bad for the girls," she said, "but I knew that I could do better by myself."

That year, Marsha attended the Treasure You retreat. She just wanted to get away for a few days, meet new people, and enjoy her family, but she got much more. In the beginning she was guarded, even refusing to take off her makeup during the pajama party. As she listened to other women's testimonies, her comfort level grew. "The anointing was in the room," she said.

The next day, after more ministering and sisterhood, she surrendered, telling God she would do whatever He had in store. "I felt like God was preparing me for an upcoming battle—like my divorce, financial struggle, difficult times, or the journey of being a single mom with four girls," she said. "I had no idea that He was getting me ready for a battle with breast cancer."

Marsha says the Treasure You retreat released something in her, and she cried like she had never cried before. "I never grieved the loss of my baby brother or grandfather," she explained. And the enormous stress from various health issues—thyroid problems, a hysterectomy, and a transfusion—had taken its toll on her well-being. "I didn't like me," she said. "I told myself that something had to change. I was running from the enemies of my past, but the Enemy was in me."

Soon after the retreat, Marsha had a mammogram. The doctor saw something suspicious and ordered an ultrasound and a biopsy. After the procedure, the doctor called Marsha into her office.

She called Emmitt and me, but her calls went to voice mail. "I told the doctor that I couldn't hear the news by myself. I thought I needed someone to hear it with me, but God had shut the phones down and told me I had Him."

The doctor revealed that she had stage two triple negative breast cancer.

After Marsha shared the news with Victor, he asked if they could stay together so he could help her through the ordeal. Family and friends stayed by Marsha's side through all of her doctor's appointments and chemotherapy and gave their unrelenting support when she had a double mastectomy.

After her reconstructive surgery and healing, Marsha said she hit rock bottom. To help cope, she began counseling, took antidepressants, and initiated the difficult process of facing her issues. Finally, after all of the physical struggles, she was ready to focus on her mental health.

"Victor and I separated and went to marriage counseling, and I started to see my husband differently. We have all sinned and fallen short in the eyes of God," she said. "I started to see him as God saw him. God holds us accountable for how we treat each other."

Today, Marsha is a four-year cancer survivor. Her marriage is still a work in progress. They participate in Marriage Matters Ministry at church. She says, "The blind can't lead the blind." Her perspective as a mother has changed and she enjoys more moments with her children than she ever did before. She realizes now how stress, negativity, and self-neglect can rob you of your happiness and power, and today, she doesn't waste any time on unhealthy pursuits.

"My life has to be productive," she said. "God gave me a second chance."

In the past, Marsha didn't believe in therapy, but she is now an advocate and has confided in a therapist throughout her health journey. She has learned to take care of her body from both a physical and an emotional standpoint. She has learned to better communicate with her husband, be more present as a mother, and live her life from a more relaxed and positive perspective.

"I'm never going back to how I lived before," she said.

Marsha is proof that when you learn to treasure yourself and regain your power, you can embrace the second chance to fulfill what God has destined for you. Marsha learned to repel negativity and stress so she could focus on being a healthier, happier, more patient and loving mother and wife.

As I reflect on my own struggles with finding my purpose and allowing time for self-care and Treasure You Moments, and as I think about Marsha's struggle with stress and health issues, I've been convinced of the direct link between stressors (both the positive and negative kind) and illness. I can even recall a time when my chiropractor, Dr. Robert Parker, explained the ways in which stress weakens the body and makes it more susceptible to illness and disease. With a history of breast cancer in my family, I don't want to have a lifestyle filled with stress, so I've learned to prioritize Treasure You Moments so I can stay focused, healthy, and whole. These moments embody all of what Treasure You is about and provide a reminder and plan to help regain and sustain power. In my mind, there are four ways that this can happen: *times of quiet and reflection, self-care, positive fellowship with others,* or *pampering and special little treats.* We all need to make it a priority to slow down, be still, and focus inward and on God. By spending time with God and taking care of ourselves, we can take care of others.

I have to take a moment to say that each type of Treasure You Moment accomplishes different things. It's important to use the right kind of Treasure You Moment for what you really need. For example, if you need time to deal with insecurity and pain, take time for quiet and reflection, not a trip to the mall. In the past, when I was stressed, sad, or feeling insecure, I'd go shopping. I'd buy beautiful things and feel great at the store and during the car ride home. But those moments of instant gratification don't last because they don't care for the soul. Shopping is just a dopamine rush that lasts for a short while. That's not real power. While shopping is a nice break, it shouldn't be a substitute for addressing issues. That's the difference. Now if I feel anxious or insecure, I take time to reflect and be quiet before God.

Let's break down the four types of Treasure You Moments as I've organized them for my life.

Times of Quiet and Reflection

There are moments in your life when you just need to get away so you can focus on yourself without interruption. I have even checked into a hotel so I could have this alone time. Earlier I shared how, after twenty years of struggle, I had a breakthrough about my mother's death. The breakthrough was exhilarating. But it was followed by exhaustion. I didn't know where to go from there. I needed to focus, and it had to be done in solitude.

When I told Emmitt I wanted to leave for the night, he didn't understand. The hotel was right up the street, so why would I leave and pay for a room when I had one at home? But as all moms know, there's getting away from the kids and the chaos, and there's *really* getting away from the kids and the chaos. If I stayed home, the kids would know exactly where I was. They'd knock on my door and come in. (I, like most other moms, can't even go to the bathroom without my kids trying to get in!) I needed to be away so I could focus.

So I left for one night. I took my Bible, a candle, and my blankie and checked into the hotel. Once in my room, I lit my candle and got into bed. I prayed, read God's Word, and relaxed. I laid on the bed in silence. I read *The Freedom of Letting Go: Overcoming Fear and Apprehending Faith*, written by my friend Melani. I didn't watch television or chat on the phone. For one day, I focused on understanding the message God gave me in prayer group regarding my mother's death. When I awoke the next day, I felt restored and rested.

When you need a day of solitude, you don't have to retreat to a hotel. You can go to the home of a friend or family member and ask to stay in a guest room for the night. If I had to choose a quiet place to stay right now, I'd call my spiritual mentor, Cathy. Her home has a peacefulness that creates the perfect ambience for reflection. If you know someone who owns a beach house, cabin, or second home, ask for the keys for one night. Even if an entire twenty-four-hour period is too demanding, take a morning or afternoon to be alone. On a beautiful day, I go to the park or take a walk. There's a pond near my house; I love to go there and sit because I find being near water to be refreshing and relaxing. I love to look at the trees and all of God's creations. It's in those quiet moments that I find revelations.

If you live near trails, go on a hike. Take a bike ride. If you're in the city, visit a bookstore or the coffee shop. You can have plenty of Treasure You Moments without spending a dime. Take time to be alone, connect with God, think about life, and count your blessings.

Self-Care

We must take time to focus on self-care, even when our busy lives mean we are running in many different directions. As we take care of everyone else—drive the kids to school, care for elderly parents, volunteer at church—often we forget about ourselves. Why do we do this? And when we do have a few moments to ourselves, why do we feel guilty? If we aren't healthy, focused, and in a good place, everyone will suffer. This example is used all the time, but I love it. Think of what the flight attendant says upon takeoff: *In the event of an emergency, place the oxygen mask on yourself first, and then help someone else.* I've learned that if I don't take the time to care for my body and mind, I'm nothing for my family or ministry. So I make sure I go to the chiropractor. I get regular massages. I exercise. And I rest. Just this morning I woke up, saw the kids off to school, and then went back to bed. After a busy two weeks I'm exhausted, and I know my hubby and kids are going to want me to be focused and refreshed for the weekend, so I decided to take a few hours to catch up on my rest. I turned my phone off, let the most important people know where I was, and slept for three hours. When I woke up, nothing had changed. The earth was still turning. No one outside of the few people I told even knew I'd shut down. I share this to say that it's okay to take some time to just sleep so you can recharge. Listen to what your body needs and nurture it.

Self-care includes the practical things we must do to stay healthy but sometimes overlook, such as making regular health and wellness visits. From annual gynecological visits to yearly mammograms, we must always prioritize these appointments. I like to remind people that early detection of the most common diseases, such as breast cancer and ovarian cancer, is the key to survival. This is exactly why regular exams are critical to your health.

To help me stay on track, I designated a month to schedule all of my appointments. With a personalized health month, I know that I'm not overlooking anything, and I don't have to try to remember the last time I had a physical. Once I schedule my appointments, I ask each doctor's office to call with a reminder, then put the dates into my smartphone and set a reminder. As parents, we make sure our kids make every dental visit and well-child/baby appointment. We need to make that same effort for ourselves.

Now, I understand that for some women it's hard to find even an hour to be alone. When I was a single mother, those moments were few and far between. But I knew there were certain appointments I had to attend, so I'd ask my sister or friends for help. Sometimes my friends and I would do time trade-outs. For example, one of my good friends was living with me when she was going through a challenging time. In turn, she would watch Jasmin as I went to acting class. Or I'd agree to watch a friend's child in exchange for her watching mine another day. Look for opportunities to trade time so you can focus on self-care.

Positive Fellowship With Others

Sometimes you just want to laugh and cut loose. I love getting together with girlfriends for lunch, a sleepover at a hotel, or a spa day. When I'm with my girls, we eat, giggle, and reflect, and these times are some of the best in my life.

Pampering and Special Little Treats

Even if you don't have a lot of time to spend alone, you can honor yourself with pampering or treats. When I really want a calorie splurge, I go to an ice-cream parlor and order a banana split. Then I sit outside and eat and people-watch. For me, this is the ultimate Treasure You Moment!

If you love chocolate, treat yourself! Craving a donut? Then have it. If you have time for a massage, manicure, or pedicure, schedule it right away. Give yourself little rewards because you deserve it.

Treasure You Moments are about giving attention to our bodies, minds, and spirits. By treasuring ourselves, we're better equipped to tackle life's challenges, live out our second chances, and enjoy every one of life's blessings that God has intended for us.

Power Points

- By taking care of ourselves, we can better take care of others.
- When you do things that you aren't called to do, you are pulling focus away from what God has assigned to you.
- When you treasure yourself and focus on what God wants you to do, you won't have time to feel jealous or bitter, or compare yourself to others.

Power Prompters

- What Treasure You Moment would you like to have?
- What Treasure You Moment have you found to be revealing, special, or even life changing?
- What dream or goal do you want to fulfill? Ask your spouse, a friend, or family member for support.

FOURTEEN

Making the Most of Your Second Chance

Second chances are one of the most beautiful and awesome gifts that God can give us. Through second chances, we can create and inspire, grow and forgive, learn and love—again and again.

It is through a second chance that we can begin a new relationship with Christ, start a new career, find love again, have a family, impact others' lives, or enjoy life to the fullest. The possibilities are endless. All of the stories and examples in this book were shared to demonstrate the beauty and impact of second chances. I hope you feel inspired and motivated. I know I do.

I've shared with you how Treasure You evolved out of my own personal misery into a ministry and organization focused on helping women and bringing them closer to God. It fills my heart and spirit to tell you that we have been so fortunate to touch the lives of thousands of people since we began this journey in 2008. More than 57,000 people have attended Treasure You retreats and events or been present for the speeches that I've been so fortunate to deliver. Through Treasure You's emergency assistance program and other organizations, we have been able to support more than 25,000 women. And as a testament to the power of social media, more than 100,000 people viewed a live stream of the event I hosted with Robin Roberts, "Celebrating Second Chances with Overcomers." The support for Treasure You has been incredible. I take no credit for any of this success. Remember, I was the girl who thought no one would show up to my first Treasure You retreat. But just look at what God can do! He is amazing.

On this journey, I have witnessed testimonies that made me cry, cheer, and celebrate. . . . And through it all, I've seen wonderful women overcome adversity, challenges, and suffering to emerge brighter, bolder, and better than before.

I am honored to share each of their stories.

Throughout my life, I've always had a heart to help people, and God gave me a second chance to do it. In 2013, I began my two-year journey through ministry school because I felt a call to a deeper level of study of God's Word for ministry. There were classes, exams, practicums, and ceremonial training. I was a dedicated student because I wanted to be equipped to minister correctly, with knowledge, training, and the Word of God so He could use me to the greatest extent possible. Now that I'm a licensed minister, I feel that I'm a stronger vessel for God.

As I hit my stride in my forties, I see things that weren't clear to me before. One of those things is the way second chances enrich and strengthen our relationships with others, and most important, with the Lord. This pattern wasn't evident to me when I was in my twenties and thirties, but now things are crystal clear: We go through things to get better and stronger, to be closer to Him, and to help impact others for a life with Christ. Without struggle, you can't have compassion, relate to others, or understand where someone is coming from. For the majority of us, if we didn't go through sufferings or trials, we wouldn't get down on our knees and pray. Every time I suffer, I grow closer to Christ.

> Not only so, but we also glory in our sufferings, because we know that suffering produces perseverance; perseverance, character; and character, hope. And hope does not put us to shame, because God's love has been poured out into our hearts through the Holy Spirit, who has been given to us.
>
> Romans 5:3–5

Suffering is essential to the human condition. When we face conflict, work through it, endure, and emerge, we are more compassionate, forgiving, and inspired.

When we come through struggle, we are stronger, healthier, and happier.

Now that I've written this book, I see second chances everywhere. My husband and I recently met with a woman named Erin Botsford, who specializes in asset protection. Now, whenever I have to talk about finances, I dread it! (I'm not a numbers girl—I'm a Treasure You girl!) But as soon as Erin started her presentation and shared what led her down this career path, I saw the beauty of second chances. By the end of the meeting, I was in tears and asked if she would share the ways in which she turned her own suffering and trials into a second chance. When you hear how she got to where she is today, you will see why she has dedicated her career to helping people protect their financial assets, and how her belief in God got her through unimaginable tragedy.

Erin grew up in a modest home in Illinois with her five brothers and sisters. It was the 1960s, and her father was a college professor. When her father decided to move the family to San Diego to pursue a career dream, he borrowed against his teacher's pension. Months later, he died of a heart attack, leaving his family in poverty. His death also meant Erin's mother, who at forty-seven had never had a formal job, was forced to rely on her six kids to help make ends meet. Erin raked leaves and baby-sat, and when she was old enough, she got a job at McDonald's. One day on her way to work, Erin's car collided with a motorcycle. The eighteen-year-old driver, who had never ridden a motorcycle before, was speeding. Four days later, the teen died from head injuries.

The trauma and guilt of the teen's death proved too much for Erin. She felt staring eyes and heard whispers wherever she went. Twice she attempted suicide. It wasn't long after the teen's funeral that Erin was charged with involuntary manslaughter. When Erin and her mother met with an attorney, he told the family that Erin needed to plead guilty because they didn't have enough money for her defense. "This is purely a matter of economics," the lawyer said. At just sixteen years old, Erin thought her life was over. "That was the day I realized that money buys choices," Erin said.

Fortunately, because her parents had purchased their house, Erin's mother could take a mortgage against it to pay for the legal fees. They went to court, and the jury found Erin not guilty. Relief washed over her, but it was short-lived. Three weeks after the criminal trial, there was a civil case. This time, Erin's family had the support and backing of their insurance company, and the company's representatives were eventually able to reach a settlement with the teen's family.

Throughout the ordeal, Erin was in the news, and the negative attention was agonizing. "I was broken," she said. But when a young man named Bob saw Erin's picture in the paper, he didn't see a killer. He saw his future wife. "To everyone in the small town, I was still the girl who killed that boy," Erin said. "He knew different. He wanted to date me for *me*. This was a turning point. We quickly fell in love."

Unfortunately, that's when her financial demise struck. Throughout her teenage years, Erin worked and saved, and by the time she was twenty years old, she had $22,000 in the bank. She bought her first condo with a $3,000 down payment and gave $19,000 to a stock broker to invest on her behalf. It wasn't long before Erin had lost it all. She vowed to learn about money and finances so that what happened in her twenties wouldn't happen to her again.

Erin and Bob married in 1979, and because Bob was a fighter pilot, they moved seventeen times in the first fourteen years of their marriage. Erin looked at each move as a chance to reinvent herself and put even more distance between herself and the small-town accident. Although she was raised Catholic, Erin said her relationship with God was in name only. Then one day in 1983, as she sat at home alone, pregnant with her son, she watched Billy Graham on TV. In that moment, Erin got on her knees and prayed. She then ordered a book from the show, *The Power of Positive Thinking.* When the book arrived, Erin asked Bob to read a few pages. He did, and then got down on his knees and prayed.

In time, they committed themselves fully to Christ.

The couple prayed regularly, asking for three specific things. Eventually, Erin says, all three requests were granted. "I think God is the most gracious to baby Christians," she said. "It strengthened our faith and began an adventure for us that is unbelievable."

It wasn't until 1992 that Erin shared her story with anyone. She was working with a couple who had just retired, and when she told them about her financial and personal struggles, she was met with hugs and empathy. "People want to work with authentic people," she said. "I tell my story not to be manipulative, but because everyone's got pain in their life. Being authentic is sharing in humanity with people."

Today, Erin has made the most of her second chance by helping others protect their financial assets so they won't endure the struggles that her family did. She even wrote a book to help people called *The Big Retirement Risk: Running Out of Money Before You Run Out of Time.* Her story is one of perseverance, grace, and faith.

"When you are going through tough times, it is often impossible to see how things could ever work out for good. But God is faithful and His promise in Romans 8:28 ("And we know that in all things God works for the good of those who love him, who have been called according to his purpose") always comes to pass. Sometimes it takes decades to connect the dots and see how God works things out, but He *always* does. More important, when you have that confidence, it makes it easier to go through tough things because you know the One True God is true to His promises."

I've talked to hundreds of women about their second chance, and I've seen a beautiful trend emerge. People who make the most of their second chance want to share their stories with others to inspire and encourage faith. They want to help people who are in similar situations by creating an organization, lending a hand, or offering support.

During the "Celebrating Second Chances with Overcomers" event, I had the opportunity to honor Marla Avery. Her story will move you to see the beauty of faith and endurance, even when a person is put to the test time and time again.

In 2008, after a diagnosis of ocular melanoma, Marla had her left eye removed.

"The next morning, my dad, my sister, and her husband, Jason, came into my room dressed like pirates! The big joke before surgery was that I would become a true pirate. My family will never know how great that made me feel. To see my daddy dressed up like Jack Sparrow was priceless. I will always remember the calls, cards, and love from friends and family, even friends I hadn't seen or spoken to since high school. . . . That was a beautiful time to see how God was working in my life."

When it was time for Marla's bandages to be removed, she hadn't yet received a donor eye, so the surgeon had to take a plastic ball, wrap it in synthetic tissue, and insert it into the eye socket. "The first time I saw my new eye, I freaked out and lost it, ending up sobbing. I can remember being very weak in the knees and almost passing out."

Marla worried about what others would think, and feared her fiancé, Stephen, would find her unattractive. "It's your heart I'm seeking, not looks or what you can do for me," she recalls him saying. "Marla, God knows your heart!"

It was several weeks before Marla could see an ocularist for her eye prosthesis. But when the day finally came, she was so excited. "I had been through a lot in such a short time," she shared. "I had been in the cosmetic industry since 1991, and I was all about helping others feel beautiful. I wasn't feeling like I could ever go back after my eye removal. Who would listen to me?"

But that afternoon, Marla had a beautiful new eye. "I was walking on air when I left the ocularist's office. He will never know what he did for me that day."

Eventually Marla returned to the cosmetics industry for a short while. "God gave me the gift of sharing my journey and showing people that beauty comes from His grace."

Marla went on to marry Stephen, and they had a daughter. But just seven weeks after her birth, Marla received terrible news: The ocular melanoma had metastasized to her liver, and there were three tumors. Marla made an appointment with a renowned oncologist. "All I could think about while waiting to speak with the doctor was that I can't die. I have a beautiful life. It took me a while to get here. I remember saying, 'Lord, I want to live. Please show me your mercy and grace.'"

The doctor recommended a new procedure called chemo catheter embolism, which would target the tumors with chemotherapy. "I had been praying with many friends and had been prayed over by the elders of our church," she said. "We prayed that God would be over my doctor and her team as they made decisions on the right treatment, but with cancer of any type, it is a hit-or-miss when trials are involved. I had decided that the Lord had this. I was going to use every inch of faith I had to get me through this."

Over the next eight months, Marla had eight cycles of treatment. In the wake of the treatment, Marla had a TIA (transient ischemic attack, which is a mini stroke) and Bell's palsy. She recovered and things seemed to be fine, but then the cancer reappeared in 2013 in her liver. Marla fought back with a treatment called radiofrequency ablation. Today, she is in remission.

Marla has triumphed over cancer three times and has gone on to graduate from a two-year Bible Training Center for Leaders at Denton Bible Church, experience her first mission trip to Nicaragua, and speak at an Ocular Melanoma Foundation conference.

"Why do women of God like me doubt?" Marla asked. "He shows up at high noon all over our lives. This is why His name is Comforter, and we will always need comforting."

To triumph over cancer three times is a tremendous feat. And to recover from health issues to go on to participate in life in the ways Marla has done is making the most of a second chance. I want to tell you about another incredible woman, Charlotte Judd, who turned a lifelong struggle with heart problems into a second chance at life.

Charlotte was twenty-one years old when her doctors told her she needed a heart transplant. She had battled a congenital heart condition since she was just three months old. Growing up, she had to sit out on many of the things healthy children could do: running, dancing, riding roller coasters . . . Her condition had been controlled by medicine, but her health deteriorated. "I had undergone a procedure that was supposed to help correct the problem, and just before Christmas I was scheduled to have a pacemaker/AICD implanted in my body so that I could return to college until spring break, at which time I would go back to the hospital and have the procedure completed. During the placement of the pacemaker/AICD device, I went into cardiac arrest and ended up on life support. The doctors quickly determined that my heart was like a ticking time bomb," Charlotte said.

Charlotte was forced to remain in the hospital, but in spite of her rare heart condition, she didn't meet any of the requirements to be placed on the transplant waiting list. She was stuck. She had to stay in the hospital throughout the holidays.

"My doctors had to go to the board more than once to get me approved for the transplant list. During this time, my family and I (I am an only child) planned my funeral just in case."

On February 6, 2003, good news came: Charlotte was placed at the top of the transplant wait list. Twenty days later, she received her new heart. On March 15, 2003, she left the hospital.

"Sustaining myself during this waiting period was easy most of the time because I am a positive and grateful-for-what-I-have kind of person. I knew God had a plan for me. I didn't know what the plan was, but I knew it was a good one."

Charlotte says her second chance came that day in February when she got her new heart. "It was a bittersweet moment because I knew what had to have happened for me to get a heart, but I promised myself and the donor family that I would do the best I could with this gift of life."

She says that every day since she walked out of the hospital is literally a second chance for her.

With her new heart, Charlotte is able to do things she always wanted to. She completed her bachelor's degree and went on to receive a master's degree in 2008. Today, Charlotte works as a counselor so that she can "show others that they too can get a second chance," she says.

And what about those activities that were once forbidden? She took her second chance and literally ran with it. Charlotte has completed more than fifteen 5K races and four half marathons.

"I say a prayer at every starting line I cross to honor my donor family, who, in their darkest hour, gave me the best gift I could ever get."

What is the second chance you want in your life? Or have you been given a second chance that you have yet to embrace and act on? Don't let fear or the Enemy hold you back. Erin, Marla, Charlotte, and all of the other brave women who've opened their hearts to share their stories will tell you that courage and faith will take you to great places.

I want to share my tips for making the most of your second chance.

1. Put God First

Trust in the Lord and seek Him first.

Matthew 6:33 says, "Seek first his kingdom and his righteousness, and all these things will be given to you as well."

I pray every morning. As soon as I'm awake, God is my first thought of the day. If my mind strays to the task of the day, I redirect it back to God. I ask Him to help me keep Him first in my thoughts.

2. Make Second Place Your First

After being named first runner-up for Miss USA (or "second loser," as I call it jokingly), I started seeing myself as "just the first runner-up." Every time I'd lose an opportunity, I'd beat myself up. I felt like I wasn't good enough to win, or else I would've gotten first place. I allowed this mentality to affect other opportunities in my life. But, for real? This was *one pageant*. I allowed this one night and a panel of judges who sat for two hours determine the next twenty years of my life? I didn't want to allow one evening to have that much power over my mind and spirit.

I finally realized there's great power to being second place. It has kept me humble and gracious. When you win all the time, you don't appreciate it. But when you lose, you work harder the next time and appreciate first place when it comes. To be honest, I'm Miss Humble now! (And I love my title.)

I've learned that if the door closes, it's for a reason, and God has a great opportunity for us somewhere else. God always knows best. Find strength in second place.

Matthew 19:26 says, "Jesus looked at them and said, 'With man this is impossible, but with God all things are possible.'"

3. Push Past Your Fear

Treasure You would never have been created if I'd given in to my fears. Fear comes from the Enemy. Faith comes from God. When you choose faith, you resist fear. You have to push past your fears and the things that the Enemy puts in your mind. When you hear the Enemy say things like, "You're not good enough! You'll never get well! You'll never have enough money!" it's all against what God says. God is a healer. He wants us to prosper and be blessed. We should follow our faith, not what the Enemy says about us.

I'll never forget visiting Lakewood Church one Sunday when Pastor Joel Osteen was ministering an "I am" sermon. From that sermon, I took away an important lesson that I use when the Enemy comes at me with words of fear and doubt: I come back at him with words of faith. I tell him, "I am a conqueror." "I am healed." "I am strong." "I am good enough." "I am smart." "I am beautiful." "I am blessed."

Psalm 139:14 says, "I praise you because I am fearfully and wonderfully made; your works are wonderful, I know that full well."

4. Stay Above It All

Stay out of the weeds. The Enemy wants to keep us distracted. I used to get so caught in the weeds of things and worry whether someone was talking about me or didn't like me. But it doesn't matter. During my last "Second Chance" event, Robin Roberts made a statement that what other people think about her is their business . . . not hers. That thought stayed with me. It took more than forty years for me to learn this, and I hope some of you get there a lot sooner!

Put people's opinions of you away, and think about what God thinks about you. When you focus on what others think, you're making idols out of people, and He doesn't like that. He's a jealous God.

Deuteronomy 4:24 says, "For the Lord your God is a consuming fire, a jealous God."

Another area that concerns me is the way that some women treat each other and talk about each other. I can remember one day watching a reality show I swore I'd never watch. I got so caught up in it, by the end I was in tears because of all the mistreatment and hurt being caused by gossip and rumors. I saw the importance of watching the words we speak about others, and why we all must stay out of the weeds. It's important as women that we keep lifting each other up, loving on one another, and providing safe havens. During some of my most devastating and delicate moments, it was a woman who helped me through. Let's make a commitment to watch how we talk about each other, and let's stay above it all.

Proverbs 16:28 says, "A perverse person stirs up conflict, and a gossip separates close friends."

5. Embrace the Journey

Embrace the ups and downs. When there are great times, rejoice and be happy and give God praise. In bad times, still rejoice and give Him thanks. Whatever you're going through, the good or the bad, be confident that it will make you better and stronger, equip you to help others, and bring you closer to the Lord.

First Thessalonians 5:18 says, "Give thanks in all circumstances; for this is God's will for you in Christ Jesus."

It is my dream that this book provides you with hope, motivation, and inspiration. I want you to know that no matter what you've been through, or what you'll go through in the future, our God gives *second chance* after *second chance* after *second chance*!

Power Points

- We go through things to get better and stronger, to be closer to Him, to impact others, and to help lead others to Christ.
- It is through a second chance that we can accomplish our goals to begin a new career journey, get married, have a family, enjoy life to the fullest, and fulfill our purpose and destiny.

- We have a God who loves us and gives us second chance after second chance.

Power Prompters

- Challenge yourself and your friends to read the Bible from beginning to end. Set a deadline and go for it. There are many Bible study programs available to accomplish this goal.
- Use your misery for ministry. Use areas that have caused you suffering as opportunities to give back and help others.
- As God gives you second chances, be more open to give second chances to others.
- Today, think about and write down the many second-chance opportunities that God has afforded you. We all have them.
- Give thanks and celebrate our God, and make the most of your second chances!

I told you to get comfortable and come on a Treasure You journey with me. As I sit here in my pj's and reflect on our Treasure You Moments together, I imagine someone telling me as a young woman twenty-some years ago, "Baby girl, life is going to be full of challenges, disappointments, hurting, suffering, and losses. But I promise you that if you lean on God and trust Him every step of the way, He will turn all of that into something super special and significant for your purpose and His glory." Please hold these words as treasures in your heart.

With love,
Your new girlfriend, Pat

Acknowledgments

This may be the longest acknowledgments section of any book written, but those who know me know that I have learned and been guided by so many people throughout my life. I have done my best to recognize those who have given me support, confidence, and love in forming the foundation of who I am today and also in writing this book.

To God Be the Glory! Without a doubt, God has been the inspiration for this book, giving me second chances in my own life over and over again, and the opportunity to be a vessel to save souls for His glory.

My hubby, Emmitt, or "Baby" as I call him, has been unfailing in his support of my ministry and philanthropic work. When it comes to giving help, hope, and opportunity to others, this is one of the areas where our hearts connect. I appreciate how determined he is and how hard he works to support our family and to give me the freedom to minister to others. He is my love and treasure.

Thank you to my five beautiful children: Jasmin, Rheagen, EJ, Skylar, and Elijah. They are such a joy in my life and one of the reasons I get up every day. Each one of them is a unique treasure and a gift that I could not have ever imagined. I thank them for their kisses, hugs, unconditional love, and patience. I have truly been blessed to be their mommy.

Thank you to my father, Henry; mother, Mildred (deceased); and sister, Pam Southall, who provided a strong family foundation to love others and dream big no matter the circumstances. A special heartfelt thank-you to Irma Anderson (Sweet Angel), who came into my family's life as a soul mate to my father after my mother passed and has loved him, my sister, and me as if we all were her own.

I have the best "in-loves" in the world, who have proven over and over again why we are not "in-laws." Thank you, Daddy Puddin, Mimi, Marsha (Tia Poo) and Victor, Eric, Emory, and in memoriam, Emil.

My Auntie Cherron and Uncle Malcom, Uncle Larry, my godmother Aunt Mildred, and Uncle Allen (deceased) have been there for me in every way. I'm grateful they have supported me and cheered me on no matter what.

Bishop T.D. and First Lady Serita Jakes and the Potter's House family have given me leadership, mentorship, and love, and also provided an environment that has fostered my spiritual growth. I'm not the same woman I was when I joined our church in 1999. Thanks for a church home where I can be inspired, find my purpose, be fed the Word of God, laugh, cry, and grow.

My spiritual mentor and sister, Elder Cathy Moffitt, taught me the importance of going to God's Word for direction. She has listened to me tirelessly for hours and coached me through the Scriptures as I have searched for answers. Cathy has mentored me through almost every situation in my adult life, and for her encouragement, I am so grateful to God.

Thank you to Tara Jackson, my best friend (BFF) for over twenty years and mother of my godbaby, Josiah. Thanks for being my secret keeper and teaching me the importance of vulnerability and how to be a "real" girlfriend.

My dear "ride-or-die chick" friend, Millicent Finney, has supported and undergirded all of my dreams and God-given assignments. I thank God for our countless hours together dreaming and laughing over the years. We are family in every sense of the word.

Many thanks to Martin and family members Rae, Robert, Ursula, Debbie, and Wanda for giving our relationship a second chance and showing that second chances are possible even after divorce.

My "Dear Brother" Darryl Jarvis, Cousin Ray (Cory) Daniels, Valerie Chandler, and Sheree Smith Fletcher were my family away from home during my time living in L.A.—and they are still in my life today. Without them I could not have made it through some of the most difficult years of my life.

Sandy Hutchinson, my first mentor; Kim Johnson, Miss Virginia USA Director and dear friend; and the Nicewonder family have been angels in my life.

Every woman needs a great group of girlfriends who not only laugh, share, cry, eat, and celebrate, but most important, pray together. Sherice Brown, Celia Drummond, Millicent Finney, Tammy Franklin, Joy Hill, Melani Ismail, Sara Miller, Donna Richardson, and Shelia Stoutmire—you are the perfect reflection of true girlfriends.

When I was lost in Los Angeles in the mid-1990s, Bishop Noel Jones and his assistant, Marjorie Duncan, took me in to the family of Greater Bethany Community Church (now known as the City of Refuge), provided me a safe place to worship, and gave me an opportunity to give my life to the Lord. My heart will forever be thankful for the love shown by them and the church community.

Reverend Joe B. Fleming, Mrs. Johnnie M. Fleming, and co-pastor Joseph Fleming provided me a Christian foundation through Third Baptist Church of Portsmouth, Virginia.

Governor Douglas Wilder and the state of Virginia gave me my first opportunity after college as a governor's fellow—my first job experience out of college. This opportunity opened my mind to the possibilities of what was in front of me.

The Western Branch High School and James Madison University communities provided me not only a scholastic foundation but a sense of social community that will last a lifetime.

My Delta Sigma Theta Sorority sisters showed me the importance and power of having other women in my life and gave me my strong sense of responsibility to the community.

Simi Juneja and Pamela Benson Owens both shared revelation and inspiration during the journey of writing this book. Their words were gentle nudges that guided me.

Werner Scott and Tina Piermarini—I offer my thanks for seeing "second chances" in my life and as a part of my future message.

My Treasure You sisters and community have given me the opportunity to do what I love most—loving other women and giving them hope by renewing their spirits after they've overcome life's setbacks and circumstances.

There are two couples who have inspired my husband and me to utilize our platform and resources to provide second-chance opportunities for others. Julie Chrysten and Dwight Opperman (deceased), Jan Miller and Jeff Rich . . . you are angels on earth.

The team at Dupree Miller (my book agency), led by Jan Miller and Nena Madonia, have proven that if I am authentic to my story and myself, I can make an impact on other women's lives through the written word. Thanks for giving me an opportunity and time to grow in order to find my voice and write my first book.

The team at Bethany House and Baker Publishing Group, including Kim Bangs and Ellen Chalifoux, have shown me patience and grace while keeping us on schedule. Thank you to Laurie Wegman, who captured the heart of my voice, added other women's second-chance stories to mine, and bundled them neatly in a powerful package that will speak to women needing a second chance.

The team of Pat Smith Enterprises and EJ Smith Enterprises, Pat & Emmitt Smith Charities, and Treasure You have worked with and loved me through all of our projects. Without the support of the Smith family household team, I could never have been all that God would have me to be. The encouragement of Ronelle Ianace, Marge Irwin, Michelle Irwin, Jessica Garza, Leslie Boysen, Nina Jones, Aurora Perez, Rocio Leonetti, and Stephanie Powell has kept me going when life got in the way and when it was hard for me to see the end of the road. They protected me, fueled me, and kept the engines running until I could get back in the driver's seat again and cross the finish line. I will forever be grateful for such an amazing team.

And finally, I am so grateful for the bravery and transparency of the more than twenty women whose stories of second chances are included in this book. These women inspire me with their hearts to reach others and encourage their second chances in life.

About the Author

Pat Smith was the first African-American woman to win the Miss Virginia USA title and first runner-up of the 1994 Miss USA Pageant. Marrying Emmitt Smith catapulted Pat into the world of Cowboys Nation, philanthropic endeavors, and raising a family. Now with five kids from prekindergarten to college, Pat Smith strives to achieve the optimum balance of celebrity and normality with her Hall of Famer husband by her side. Her faith, family, and "girl's girl" attitude make her a breath of fresh air.

Pat has dedicated her career to raising awareness about issues affecting women and children. Currently, she serves as the CEO of Pat Smith Enterprises and founder and CEO of Treasure You and co-founder of Pat and Emmitt Smith Charities.

Pat lost her mother to breast cancer while preparing for the Miss Virginia competition. That tragedy, along with other setbacks, inspires her to minister to other hurting women through her nonprofit Treasure You.

Treasure You is dedicated to giving hope, resources, and the possibilities for second chances to women who have experienced life's setbacks and difficult circumstances.

Pat accepted a call to minister in 2012 and now is a licensed minister through The Potter's House School of Ministry founded by Bishop T.D. Jakes.

Through all of this, Pat still finds time to manage a successful career as a television personality and inspirational speaker. In March 2016, the Oprah Winfrey Network (OWN) aired the TV special "Mrs. & Mr. Smith," which chronicled the lives of Pat and Emmitt. Her television career highlights include serving as a correspondent for *Extra*, the Emmy Award–winning entertainment news program; guest host for *Access Hollywood*; host of "Treasure You" on *Good Morning Texas*; host of *Keep the Faith*; host of *D: The Broadcast*; and recurring roles and guest appearances on such primetime hits as *Beverly Hills, 90210*; *Sunset Beach*; and *The Wayans Bros*. She addresses groups of all sizes with her inspirational messages including being a featured speaker for women's groups through the Women of Faith tour, The Potter's House, and Lakewood Church in Houston.

Pat received a bachelor's degree in journalism from James Madison University. She and Emmitt reside in Dallas with their children.